Implementing Response to Intervention in Reading Within the Elementary Classroom

Phillip M. Weishaar
Southern Illinois University, Edwardsville

Mary Konya Weishaar
Southern Illinois University, Edwardsville

Boston   Columbus   Indianapolis   New York   San Francisco   Upper Saddle River
Amsterdam   Cape Town   Dubai   London   Madrid   Milan   Munich   Paris   Montreal   Toronto
Delhi   Mexico City   Sao Paulo   Sydney   Hong Kong   Seoul   Singapore   Taipei   Tokyo

Vice President and Editor in Chief: Jeffery W. Johnston
Executive Editor and Publisher: Stephen D. Dragin
Editorial Assistant: Jamie Bushell
Vice President, Director on Marketing: Margaret Waples
Senior Managing Editor: Pamela D. Bennett
Operations Supervisor: Central Publishing
Operations Specialist: Laura Messerly
Art Director: Jayne Conte
Cover Designer: Suzanne Behnke
Cover Art: Fotolia
Project Management: Sudip Sinha
Composition: Aptara®, Inc.
Printer/Binder: Courier/Stoughton
Cover Printer: Courier/Stoughton
Text Font: 10/12 Times

Credits and acknowledgments borrowed from other sources and reproduced, with permission, in this textbook appear on appropriate page within text.

Every effort has been made to provide accurate and current Internet information in this book. However, the Internet and information posted on it are constantly changing, so it is inevitable that some of the Internet addresses listed in this textbook will change.

Library of Congress Cataloging-in-Publication Data
Weishaar, Phillip M.
    Implementing response to intervention in reading within the elementary classroom/Phillip M. Weishaar, Mary Konya Weishaar.
        p. cm.
    Includes bibliographical references and index.
    ISBN-13: 978-0-13-702263-8
    ISBN-10: 0-13-702263-8
    1. Reading (Elementary)—United States.   2. Response to intervention (Learning disabled children)   I. Weishaar, Mary Konya.   II. Title.
    LB1573.W45 2012
    372.4—dc22

                                                                                                    2010035983

10 9 8 7 6 5 4 3 2 1

ISBN 10:   0-13-702263-8
ISBN 13: 978-0-13-702263-8

Dedication

This book is dedicated to all of the children in the world who could benefit from Response to Intervention. It is also dedicated to our own two children, Paul and Mark Weishaar, who continue to make life interesting.

Phillip M. Weishaar

Mary Konya Weishaar

PREFACE

Response to Intervention (RtI) is a systemwide change occurring in schools throughout the United States. Several important principles of RtI include the following:

- All students can learn.
- Early intervention is helpful.
- Decisions should be made using data.
- Student progress should be monitored to guide intervention.
- Evidenced-based, validated interventions should be used as much as possible.
- Assessment to systematically screen all children to identify students who need further intervention is useful (NASDSE, 2006).

One study of the State Directors of Special Education indicated that 90% of states were in various stages of consideration or active implementation of RtI (Hoover, Baca, Wexler-Love, & Saenz, 2008). Marshall (2009) reported results of a Web-based survey of K–12 school administrators that revealed that 71% of respondents were implementing RtI. The same survey also reported that the following barriers were impeding implementation: inadequate teacher training, lack of intervention resources, and inadequate data, knowledge, and skills for tracking and charting student progress.

At the same time that schools are actively involved in planning and implementation of RtI, higher education appears to be at an initial phase of awareness and implementation of RtI. For example, one study evaluated Illinois higher-education course syllabi in special education and found that preservice teacher preparation in the use of scientifically based reading instruction was less than adequate (Reschly, Holdheide, Smartt, & Oliver, 2008). Scientifically based reading instruction, as defined by the study authors, included several components of RtI—e.g., universal screening for all children and progress monitoring for readers who struggle. This study indicated that, in Illinois, 74% of higher-education special education course syllabi reviewed did not show evidence of teaching progress monitoring, and 77% did not show evidence of teaching about universal screening. Similar studies concluded that most graduates of teacher-preparation programs were not well prepared in implementing scientifically based reading instruction (Smartt & Reschly, 2007; Walsh, Glaser, & Wilcox, 2006).

Professional standards for initial programs serving preservice teachers and advanced programs for veteran teachers support increased knowledge and skills in student assessment and data-based decision making. For example, the National Council for Accreditation of Teacher Education (NCATE) Standard 1, Element 1d, states that teacher candidates are responsible for ensuring student learning and that initial preparation of teachers requires that "teacher candidates assess and analyze student learning, make appropriate adjustments to instruction, and monitor student progress. . . ." (NCATE, 2008, p. 19). Advanced candidates are expected to "analyze student, classroom, and school performance data and make data-driven decisions about strategies for teaching and learning so that all students learn" (NCATE, 2008, p. 19). Three specialized professional associations, all of which are standards based (early childhood, elementary education, special education), include standards that address preservice teacher competency in general assessment, use of assessment for progress monitoring, and the importance of data-based decision making (National Association for the Education of Young Children, 2001; Association for Childhood Education International, 2007; Council for Exceptional Children, 2002). Similarly, the National Board for Professional Teaching Standards (n.d.) and the Interstate New Teacher Assessment and Support Consortium, or ITASC (1992), specify standards addressing assessment and progress monitoring.

There appears to be a mismatch between the speed at which public schools are planning and implementing RtI, the requirement of professional standards to include components of RtI, and the awareness level and implementation of RtI components in higher education. Public schools are moving quickly (and sometimes with little knowledge and guidance) toward implementation of RtI. At the same time, professional associations require teacher-education programs to meet stringent standards encompassing some components of RtI. However, current research suggests that higher-education institutions are not keeping pace with the preparation of RtI components in coursework and experiences. A general consensus is yet to be determined on exactly where the components of RtI are best taught in higher education and with what intensity. For example, should RtI be taught as a component of a special education and/or general education assessment course? Should RtI be taught as part of a special education and/or general education reading methods course? Should RtI be taught as a special interest workshop?

The amount of high-quality, detailed information on RtI is seemingly endless and overwhelming. Given the vast amount of available information, rapid pace of implementation within the public schools, expanding expectations placed on all teachers, and the beginning conversations within higher education, it is an overwhelming challenge to know exactly where to begin in implementing the core principles of RtI.

This book focused on two audiences: preservice teachers and inservice teachers. In higher education, this text can be used as one unit within a required course in assessment or reading methods for special and/or general education preservice teachers, or it can be spiraled with other topics throughout a semester within these courses. The text would also be beneficial for practicing teachers taking coursework at the graduate level or attending school-based inservice workshops in learning exactly what to do in implementing the essential components of RtI in reading.

This book focuses on the "bottom line," or exactly what any elementary teacher (preservice or inservice) can do to implement the essential core principles of RtI in the area of reading. Each chapter focuses on doable, clear steps for implementation. Valuable resources are also included throughout each chapter, which enrich and make implementation more meaningful and efficient. Examples and suggested activities are used throughout the chapters to enhance understanding of concepts presented. Each chapter begins with a concept map to preview the guiding principles discussed in the chapter. At the end of each chapter is a case study or two to illustrate best practice and/or less-than-best practice. The case studies help the reader apply and problem solve using concepts presented in the context of the "real world."

The intent of this book is to provide specific, clear guidance on how to implement RtI principles in reading without the advantage of substantial extra resources (money, people, etc.). The basic resources at hand are the classroom teacher, core curriculum materials, and the willingness to implement key components of RtI. We believe that any teacher can learn to implement the core principles of RtI in the area of reading. This text represents a practical, down-to-earth guide to bridge the multitude of ideas in practice, theory, and research to the real-life context of our elementary general education classrooms. By using this text within higher-education coursework or school-based inservice workshops, teachers will be better prepared to improve the quality of reading instruction for all students.

Phillip M. Weishaar, PhD
Mary Konya Weishaar, PhD

ACKNOWLEDGMENTS

We appreciate the input from our exceptional reviewers: Berttram Chiang, University of Wisconsin–Oshkosh; Kelli Esteres, Aquinas College; Todd Haydon, University of Cincinnati; Cynthia Herr, University of Oregon; John Hintze, University of Massachusetts; Chhanda Islam, Murray State University; Dana Newingham, Indiana Wesleyan University; and Jill Sharkey, University of California, Santa Barbara.

We also appreciate the expert guidance and support from our excellent editors, Ann Davis and Steve Dragin, as well as their assistants.

ABOUT THE AUTHORS

Phillip M. Weishaar was a dedicated and successful special education administrator for 28 years and a special education teacher for 6 years before becoming assistant professor in the Department of Special Education and Communication Disorders at Southern Illinois University Edwardsville in 2008. Dr. Weishaar studied and implemented many aspects of Response to Intervention beginning in the 1990s within his special education cooperative. Dr. Weishaar is an accomplished presenter, author of several articles, and coauthor of a special education administration textbook. He serves on several Illinois statewide leadership teams. His areas of interest include special education administration, systemwide change, outcome assessment, and a unitary system of special and general education. Dr. Weishaar earned a PhD in education from St. Louis University in 1984.

Mary Konya Weishaar was a special education administrator for 10 years and a special education teacher for 8 years before coming to Southern Illinois University Edwardsville in 1994. As assistant, associate, and full professor, Dr. Weishaar taught in the Department of Special Education and Communication Disorders before becoming associate dean for the School of Education in 2006. Dr. Weishaar is the author or coauthor of five textbooks, a book chapter, and numerous articles. She was the recipient of a Fulbright Senior Scholar Award to lecture in Kiev, Ukraine, in 2002. Her areas of interest include special education legal issues, assessment, international issues in special education, and the use of case studies. Dr. Weishaar earned a PhD in education from St. Louis University in 1984.

BRIEF CONTENTS

CONTENTS

Overview

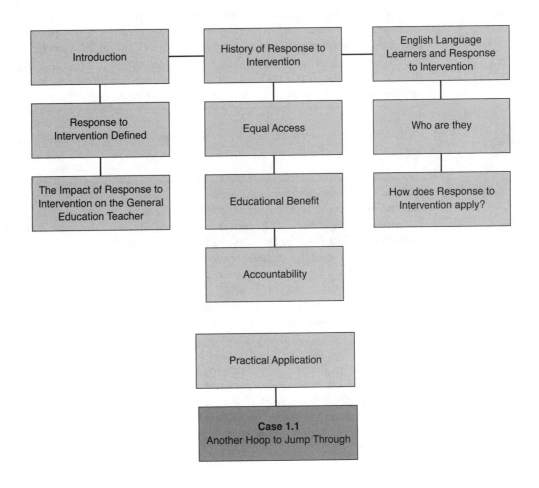

INTRODUCTION

The following scenarios describe how Response to Intervention (RtI) was perceived by two different elementary teachers. The first comes from a first-grade teacher.

> *As a first-grade teacher, I truly believe in the RtI philosophy and believe it is what we should do for all of the students we teach! RtI is what good teaching should be. It is a paradigm shift, focusing on finding out what my students' needs are and then providing solid interventions. By preparing in advance, I was organized and able to assess all students in the important areas of early reading three times this year. Most of my students, 22 out of 25, met the expected reading benchmarks for first grade, and the other 3 students needed supplementary intervention. I provided this intervention every day for these 3 students. I also assessed this group's progress in reading every other week. One student who is part of the small group also receives special education assistance. At parent conferences, I showed parents the progress their child was making. RtI has helped me document learning, differentiate instruction, and provide quality instruction. It is a challenge in my classroom to find time for assessment and small-group instruction, but it is absolutely worthwhile for every student.*

The second scenario was conveyed by a third-grade teacher in a public school, and it paints a different perspective of RtI.

> *I would never send my child to a public school. Just wait until RtI is fully implemented! It's going to be horrible! My school is already implementing RtI for reading. It's already a nightmare. The state is mandating that we "tier" our students into three "tiers." The first tier includes students who would learn anyway, regardless of teaching. The second tier includes students who will learn with a little guidance, and the third tier includes students who struggle greatly and can't learn at the same pace as the other students. As teachers, we are then required to gear our instruction to the lowest achieving, or third tier. We have to test the third tier weekly and monitor their progress. If students aren't progressing, we have to modify our instruction to yield different results . . . AND we have to do all of this without any assistance from a teacher's aid or the special education teacher. It's just crazy! As I just said, my school is having a horrible time trying to find time to do all of the testing, and we are just implementing reading this year, not reading and math. I am really frustrated that I have to do all of this work without any help—not even for the kids who struggle. Also, individualized education programs (IEPs) are being eliminated. There won't be any more IEPs. I give up—if the state has mandated RtI, it is out of my hands, and there is nothing I can do.*

These scenarios demonstrate that teacher attitudes toward students and implementation of RtI differ greatly. In the first scenario, the teacher believes that all children can learn and that student progress must be tracked and appropriate interventions that are likely to promote learning must be provided. The teacher also realizes that some students need more intensive and supplementary intervention to be successful readers. Assessing, tracking progress, and differentiating instruction are a "way of life" for this teacher. The teacher also communicates progress to parents in a clear, concrete manner.

The second scenario portrays a different picture. The teacher paints a negative picture of RtI; one that is potentially harmful to children. The scenario includes the misconception that all instruction should be focused on the lowest achieving students and that some children learn regardless of the quality of teaching. The teacher feels that it is impossible to systematically assess student progress and change instruction as needed without outside assistance. The teacher also thinks that individualized education programs for students with disabilities will be eliminated because of RtI, which is inaccurate.

Response to Intervention (RtI) Defined

RtI is based on the philosophy that all children can learn. The National Association of State Directors of Special Education (NASDSE) and the Council of Administrators of Special Education (CASE) issued a joint paper that defined RtI as "the practice of providing high-quality instruction and interventions matched to student need, monitoring progress frequently to make decisions about changes in instruction or goals and applying child response data to important educational decisions" (NASDSE, 2006, p. 3). Johnson, Mellard, Fuchs, and McKnight (2006) defined RtI as "an assessment and intervention process for systematically monitoring student progress and making decisions about the need for instructional modifications or increasingly intensified services using progress monitoring data" (p. 12). NASDSE (2006) detailed the following eight core principles of RtI:

1. All children can be taught and can learn.
2. Intervention must occur early.
3. Services are best delivered in several different "tiers."
4. For children to move from one tier to another, employing a problem-solving method is useful.
5. To the greatest extent possible, teachers should use evidence- or research-based instruction and interventions.
6. Student progress should be monitored and used to adjust instruction.
7. Data from student progress (and other sources) should be used to make decisions.
8. Assessments are typically used for three different purposes:
   - *Screening* for all students to identify those who are not progressing as expected
   - *Conducting diagnostic* or more *in-depth assessment* to determine what students can and cannot do in academic and behavior areas
   - *Monitoring progress* of students to determine if they are learning at expected rates.

Typically, schools utilize a three-tier approach when operationalizing RtI. This structure is summarized in Table 1.1.

Gersten et al. (2009) reported that there is moderate evidence supporting the practice of screening students in the early elementary grades for possible reading problems at the beginning and middle of the school year, as well as regularly monitoring the progress of students who are at risk for reading difficulty. There is strong evidence supporting the practice of providing intensive and regular intervention or instruction on at least three foundational reading skills to students who are at risk for reading difficulty. Fuchs (2007a) reported on two studies (one in reading and one in mathematics) in which students, depending on how much they improved during the fall, were randomly assigned in January to receive supplemental small-group instruction in addition to general education instruction or to receive just the standard general education instruction. In

TABLE 1.1

Tier	What Curriculum Is Used?	Where Does Instruction Occur?	Focus of Instruction and/or Intervention	Assessment Structure Used
Tier 1	Evidence-based *core curriculum*	General education setting	Focus on *all* students (successful with approximately 80% of students)	Systematic screening of all students (three or four times a year)
Tier 2	Evidence-based core curriculum plus evidence-based *small-group interventions*	Usually general education setting	Focus on *some* students (approximately 15% of students who did not meet expected benchmarks in Tier 1)	Progress monitoring (every other week)
Tier 3	Evidence-based core curriculum plus evidence-based small group interventions plus evidence-based, intensive, *individualized instruction and/ or interventions*	Both inside and outside of the general education setting	Focus on a *few* students (approximately 5% of students who did not respond to Tier 2 interventions)	Progress monitoring (weekly)

Note: Students move from one tier to another, in either direction, as appropriate, based on progress monitoring. Progress monitoring and the implementation of RtI are successful when student performance reaches 80% in Tier 1, 15% in Tier 2, and 5% in Tier 3 or better.

(*Sources:* Batsche et al., 2005; Kurns & Tilly, 2008; NASDSE, 2006; Pierangelo & Giuliani, 2008)

both studies, students who received supplemental small-group instruction achieved better than students who did not receive the additional small-group instruction.

The Impact of Response to Intervention on the General Education Teacher

"One assumption of RtI infrastructure development is that RtI is implemented by the entire building. Components can be modified and generalized to smaller units. . . ." (Kurns & Tilly, 2008). Classroom teachers *can* implement the core concepts of RtI within the classroom without a schoolwide infrastructure. First, teachers must be committed to understanding how each student functions relative to grade-level expectations. Second, teachers must hold the belief that *all* children *can* learn to read and that *all* teachers are responsible for teaching *all* children. The RtI model is for teachers who want to use data to guide instructional decision making in the general education classroom. Consider this scenario as an example of how a first-grade teacher could carry out the core components of RtI.

As a classroom teacher, my goal is for all students to be able to read. For example, as I enter my first-grade classroom on September 1, I meet my students for the first time. I will use my "core" reading curriculum to teach my students, but unless I know if they are progressing, my teaching is not informed by assessment of student progress. RtI provides me with a framework to monitor how well my students are learning to read and to know where they should be at certain points during the year. I screen all of my students in reading within the first month of school using several key reading assessments, including Letter Naming Fluency, Phonemic Segmentation Fluency, and Nonsense Word Fluency. After summarizing class-wide and individual student's results, I can see if any students are not meeting the established benchmarks. If several students show that they are experiencing difficulty, I know this early in the year and monitor their progress for about 6 weeks. Then, if these students still are not making adequate progress, I am able to intervene with these students systematically and immediately, using research-based supplemental interventions. While continually monitoring progress for several weeks, I am able to again determine how this smaller group is progressing. If an individual student needs more intensive intervention, I may immediately request more assistance. This could mean evaluation for special education eligibility.

In practice, this is the meaning of RtI within the classroom. The general education teacher is affected by the implementation of the principles of RtI in a positive way. General education teachers are accustomed to monitoring the progress of their students in formal and informal ways, so RtI may replace the time previously used for assessing progress by using more formalized and consistent data to monitor progress.

HISTORY OF RESPONSE TO INTERVENTION

The term *Response to Intervention* was first used in 2001 as part of the findings from a researcher's roundtable organized by the U.S. Department of Education Office of Special Education Programs (OSEP). The purpose of this roundtable discussion was to establish consensus regarding research on learning disabilities (National Research Center on Learning Disabilities, 2007a). Researchers agreed that the intelligence quotient/achievement discrepancy was not a necessity to identify individuals with learning disabilities and that RtI was promising in the identification of specific learning disabilities.

The Individuals with Disabilities Education Improvement Act was signed into law on December 3, 2004. The corresponding regulations specifying how the statutes are to be implemented were published on August 14, 2006. In this reauthorization of the Individuals with Disabilities Education Act (IDEA), several foundational concepts of RtI were referenced. The phrase "child's response to scientific, research-based intervention" was used in specifying how students who had specific learning disabilities could be identified.

A State must adopt, consistent with 34 CFR 300.309, criteria for determining whether a child has a specific learning disability as defined in 34 CFR 300.8(c)(10). In addition, the criteria adopted by the State:

- Must not require the use of a severe discrepancy between intellectual ability and achievement for determining whether a child has a specific learning disability, as defined in 34 CFR 300.8(c)(10);

- Must permit the use of a process based on the child's response to scientific, research-based intervention; and
- May permit the use of other alternative research-based procedures for determining whether a child has a specific learning disability, as defined in 34 CFR 300.8(c)(10).

A public agency must use the State criteria adopted pursuant to 34 CFR 300.307(a) in determining whether a child has a specific learning disability 34 CFR 300.307.

In addition, states were allowed flexibility in the use of funds allocated under the Individuals with Disabilities Education Improvement Act. States were able to use up to 15% of monies received under this law to develop and implement early-intervening services for students in kindergarten through Grade 12 (emphasizing up to Grade 3) who were not identified as needing special education services but who needed additional academic and behavioral support to succeed in general education (34 CFR 300.226 [a]–[b]).

It has been stated that educational issues are essentially political policy and social issues that reflect and form the underpinning for federal law (Turnbull & Turnbull, 2000). Weishaar (2008) suggested that during the 1960s and 1970s, the focus of legislation was on equal access, or "opening the schoolhouse doors" for all children to receive an appropriate education. Inputs into the educational system (e.g., funds) were emphasized as the primary measure of accountability. During the 1980s and 1990s, after schools were open to all children, the focus shifted to student achievement outcomes as the primary measure of accountability. During the 2000s, goals for all children, assessment of progress toward those goals, highly qualified teachers, and the use of research-based interventions served as the primary measures of school accountability. One of the primary issues addressed in the Individuals with Disabilities Education Improvement Act of 2004 was accountability for student learning. To understand how accountability and RtI were related and evolved, it is important to understand an overview of how education for students with disabilities developed.

Equal Access

SCENARIO 1 (1960)

I remember Tom as a classmate in early elementary school. It was obvious that Tom was not able to read or keep up with other children as early as first grade. When we read in our reading group aloud, Tom's face would blush when his turn came. He would look down at his reading book and stumble over easy words, while the teacher supplied unknown words. Other kids would laugh quietly as Tom read. As I recall, Tom did not receive any extra assistance in reading.

SCENARIO 2 (1971)

Joe never attended the public school. When he was a baby, his father severely abused him, throwing him against a wall. Joe had severe physical disabilities and was confined to a wheelchair. He could speak, but he could not eat or breathe on his own without oxygen. He had no use of his legs or arms and had to be tube fed. Joe was cared for in a residential facility for children with severe disabilities. He was destined to spend his entire life in an institution.

These two scenarios depict how children with disabilities were educated during the 1950s, 1960s, and 1970s, before federal laws mandated that all children receive a free and appropriate public education. In the first scenario, Tom obviously experienced significant difficulty in reading, yet he did not receive assistance. Joe, with significant physical disabilities, did not receive a formal education but was cared for in an institution. At this time, there was considerable social and political conflict and, as a result, there was a demand for equality of access to education for *all* school-age students. Until these conflicts were resolved, students placed in institutions or residential facilities were not the responsibility of public school, and most of these students did not have access to a public school education. It was not until the civil rights movement in the 1950s that schools legally became responsible for the education of all students. Although the civil rights movement focused specifically on access of African American students to integrated public schools, the movement formed the basis and provided the structure for access of students with disabilities to integrated public schools. Based on the civil rights movement, parents of students with severe disabilities argued in the courts for equal access to a public school education for their children. Case law addressing access to public school services was the impetus behind federal legislation in the mid-1960s and early 1970s to ensure access for disadvantaged students and students with disabilities. The Elementary and Secondary Education Act of 1965 addressed the need for disadvantaged youth to be educated in the public schools. The Education of All Handicapped Children Act in 1975 granted access to public schools for students with disabilities. Partly because President John F. Kennedy had a sibling with developmental disabilities, action was taken at the national level to provide services for people with disabilities. For example, the National Institute for Child Health and Human Development was established by Congress in 1962 to promote the education and well-being of people with developmental disabilities. In 1963, President Lyndon Johnson created the President's Committee on Mental Retardation. Both of these organizations remain in existence today.

Educational Benefit

SCENARIO (1985)

Lori was placed in special education for reading, math, and written language when she was in third grade. Lori was making good progress in reading and mathematics but continued to struggle with written language in sixth grade. Lori's father was unhappy with the fact that Lori was already in sixth grade and continued to have difficulty with written language. He filed for a due-process hearing, contending that the district had not provided Lori with a program that allowed her to benefit in written language. In the years between third and sixth grade, the district moved toward an outcome-oriented education. This meant that they had performance data on reading and math but did not collect data on written language. The district did not have national norms for written language, so they did not use a data-based progress-monitoring system to track her progress in written language. The school district settled the dispute with Lori's father by stating that they would collect local norms on written language and use the data to intervene and monitor progress in the same way that they had done with reading and math. The district was a member of an 11-district special education cooperative. School psychologists from the cooperative conducted screenings on written language of all sixth graders and seventh graders in all 11 districts, three times a year, to get normative data that could be used in progress monitoring for Lori during seventh grade. As a result, the district was actually able to determine Lori's functioning relative to the local norms, implement research-based interventions, and show progress for Lori over time in written language.

This scenario is an example of the focus on providing educational benefit. Lori was progressing well in reading and math, but her parents did not feel that she was making progress in written language. The school district was not collecting data about Lori's progress in written language, even though she was receiving special education services for a disability in that area.

During the 1980s, the focus on education began to change for both students with and without disabilities. For students with disabilities, the focus moved from equal access to educational benefit. Case law focused on educational benefit for students with disabilities who were receiving services in the public schools. For example, in the Supreme Court case *Board of Education of the Hendrick Hudson Central School District v. Rowley* (1982), an elementary school student with a disability was found to be receiving an appropriate education or educational benefit because she was progressing from grade to grade and was provided with specially designed instruction (special education) to meet her unique needs. The Court asked two questions in determining educational benefit: Did the school comply with the procedures under the law in special education? Was the student's individualized education plan reasonably calculated to provide educational benefit? If the answer to both questions was yes, the student was benefiting from the education provided.

Students without disabilities were perceived as underperforming compared to their foreign counterparts. A publication by the National Commission on Excellence in Education, titled *A Nation at Risk* (1983), was the result of a 2-year study. It found that students across America were performing poorly compared to students in other industrialized nations. As a result, educators began to consider school reform as a top priority. For students with and without disabilities, the focus moved from educational benefit and the status quo of American education toward accountability for the outcomes of all students.

Accountability

SCENARIO (1998)

George's individualized education plan (IEP) meeting was held in May, at the end of fifth grade. George had a learning disability, affecting his ability to read. George experienced difficulty connecting sounds to letters and could not read three-letter words even with short vowels. During the IEP meeting, the special education teacher stated that "George made good progress this year in reading. He is reading at a second-grade level and tries hard. He always completes all of his homework." George's mother asked, "What can you show me to substantiate this progress?" The teacher could not respond because there was no objective information to share that reflected his progress, other than grades.

This scenario illustrates how a special education teacher experienced difficulty specifying how she knew that her student, George, made progress. The teacher focused on the grade level of reading and the fact that George tried to succeed by completing homework.

During the 1990s, the national educational focus changed from ensuring educational benefit to accountability for student progress. In 1992, the National Association for State Boards of Education released a report, titled "Winners All: A Call for Inclusive Schools," stressing the need for teachers to be qualified to teach all students, especially students with disabilities. In 1994, the National Institute for Child Health and Human Development, which was originally created by President Kennedy, suggested that the method for determining eligibility for learning disabilities was a "wait to fail" model and that a system should be in place to identify students at risk earlier. For example, a student experiencing difficulty in reading while in kindergarten often would not display the necessary "gap" between ability and achievement to be labeled as learning disabled. This same student typically would display a larger "gap" in second or third grade, while displaying a failure to learn essential skills in reading.

At the turn of the 21st century, public school education was clearly focused on accountability for the learning of all students in all settings. The reauthorization of the 1965 Elementary and Secondary Act in 2001, called the No Child Left Behind Act (NCLB), placed penalties on schools who failed to provide state-level test scores indicating that all students were meeting or exceeding the state standards. NCLB required all schools to set high expectations for the performance of all students and held schools accountable for failure to meet the standards. The 1997 reauthorization of IDEA mandated that students with disabilities be included in state and school district assessments, as determined by the IEP team. In the 2004 reauthorization of the IDEA, called the Individuals with Disabilities Education Improvement Act, focus was on ensuring that the mandates of accountability in NCLB were enforced in IDEA. High expectations and assured access to the general curriculum were focal points of IDEIA 2004. Both NCLB and IDEA required districts to set high expectations for all students and to monitor the progress toward achieving those goals, especially for students not performing up to the expectation set by the district and state. Therefore, even though the term *Response to Intervention* was originally used for special education, it became a focus for the reform movement of all education. RtI initially was used to make certain that students with potential learning disabilities received intervention within general education as opposed to immediately referring the child for learning disabilities or special education intervention. However, this focus on learning disabilities has moved toward appropriate interventions for all children, not just children potentially identified as having a disability. RtI is now a means of ensuring that all children achieve and meet high standards.

Since the election in 2009 of President Obama, the federal government has reinforced the importance of accountability for each child's learning. One major reform effort, part of the American Recovery and Reinvestment Act of 2009, was called Race to the Top. This competitive grant initiative awarded significant funds ($4.35 billion) to states that implemented significant reforms in these four areas:

- Adopting standards and assessments that prepare students to succeed in college and the workplace and to compete in the global economy
- Building data systems that measure student growth and success and inform teachers and principals about how they can improve instruction
- Recruiting, developing, rewarding, and retaining effective teachers and principals, especially where they are needed most
- Turning around our lowest achieving schools
  (*Source: Race to the Top Program Executive Summary*, by U.S. Department of Education, 2009)

As priorities for Race to the Top applications, states had to include comprehensive education reform approaches; emphasis on science, technology, engineering, and mathematics;

innovations for improving early learning outcomes; expansion and adaptation of statewide longitudinal data systems; coordination of preschool through age 20; and school-level conditions for reform, innovation, and learning. This federal reform effort emphasized the reliance on standards, assessment of student growth and achievement, and use of data to improve student learning. These areas were also central to RtI.

ENGLISH LANGUAGE LEARNERS AND RESPONSE TO INTERVENTION

Language diversity in schools continues to increase. To illustrate, consider the following descriptive data:

- Approximately 20% of school-age students (ages 5–17) spoke a language other than English at home in 2007, and 5% had difficulty speaking English (U.S. Department of Education, National Center for Education Statistics, 2009).
- The percentage of school-age students who spoke a language other than English rose from 9% to 20% between 1979 and 2007 (U.S. Department of Education, National Center for Education Statistics, 2009).

Although the number of English language learners varies by geographical region, it is likely that most, if not all, teachers will work with children whose primary language is not English.

How do the principles of RtI apply to English language learners? Gersten and colleagues (2007) reviewed rigorous research and formulated excellent best-practice principles in *Effective Literacy and English Language Instruction for English Learners in the Elementary Grades,* a practice guide. Generally, RtI practices *can* be applied to English language learners with success. Gersten et al. (2007) suggested that there is strong evidence to support the following RtI practices:

- Screen students using English language assessments to determine if students need more intensive (tier 2) intervention in reading. An important finding suggested that it is not essential for students to display oral proficiency in English to learn to read in English. Waiting until students are proficient in English prior to assessment is too late.
- Provide systematic intervention in small groups for English language learners who are, based on screening, at risk for developing reading difficulty.
- Monitor student progress to determine the effect of intervention.

Today, the general education teacher is held accountable for the progress of all students for whom he or she is responsible. General education teachers need to have access to and expertise in implementing assessment (for screening and progress monitoring) and research-based interventions that do not add unnecessary responsibilities to the already full plate.

The intent of this book is to assist teachers in meeting the accountability mandates of federal and state laws within the constraints of everyday, real-life teaching.

Because the area of reading is integral to the success of children in school, the focus of this book is on reading, even though other important areas contribute to success. In addition, this book is focused on elementary education (kindergarten through sixth grade). Teachers who are skilled in collecting student data, analyzing data, applying interventions, monitoring progress, and adjusting instruction based on data and outcomes in reading can learn to apply these same skills to mathematics and written language.

PRACTICAL APPLICATION

CASE 1.1

Another Hoop to Jump Through

I am a third-year first-grade teacher in a small elementary school serving kindergarten through second-grade students. Today, teachers in our school attended an after-school in-service. In a memo from the superintendent, it was stated that our building principal and special education director wanted to meet with all teachers in our elementary school to describe some changes that would affect our responsibilities as general education teachers. As I walked into the cafeteria, my initial thought was, *Oh no. Not another hoop to jump through to get kids into special education.*

At the meeting, the special education director began by stating, "Too many students are placed in special education. In fact, so many students have been identified with disabilities that the state school board questions whether they even have a disability. In some cases, general education teachers are not well qualified to teach the subject that they are teaching, so when the student doesn't understand what is taught, the teacher automatically refers the student to special education." This comment really angered me, but I held my composure. The director continued by stating, "General education teachers usually do not use the best or most appropriate techniques or materials to teach students. What I mean is that teachers should only use research-based materials and techniques."

At this point, the noise level in the room became loud and many of my colleagues began to ask questions. "What were we supposed to use?" "These are the books we selected, and no one said they weren't good."

The director responded, "I can't tell you specifically what you should be using, but I do think that what you are using is not always research based. It is clear that you will have to change." The director continued, "General education teachers need to keep better records on how students learn. All teachers should know how every student learns in class, and if any students are not learning as expected, then you will be required to prove that you are qualified to teach the subject and that research-based materials and techniques are used." At this point, some teachers walked out of the meeting.

During the next part of the meeting, our building principal took over. He stated, "Teaching as you know it will change! You will not be able to refer a child to special education unless you can first prove that you are qualified, use research-based techniques, provide special instruction to those who struggle, and keep charts on the performance of students who are experiencing difficulty. You cannot refer a child to special education until it is clear that you tried to teach the child first and failed. Finally, I have to tell you that research indicates that special education does not always help a student." Our principal then talked about how we, as teachers, would be responsible for assessing our students' progress. We would form a building-based team to discuss how students who struggled were progressing. The team would suggest research-based strategies for the student. Only when these strategies did not work would a student be referred for special education. Very few teachers were listening to our principal and the special education director at that point.

Wow! I thought as I left the cafeteria. *We have to fail as teachers before we can refer a child to special education.* I could not believe that our principal and the special education director questioned my professionalism and that of my colleagues. We were told that students needed to stay in the general education classroom until the teacher failed to teach the student, and only then could the special education teacher work with the student. If this is what education was going to look like in the future, I wanted no part of it.

Questions

1. Describe RtI based on this scenario. Is this an accurate representation? Why or why not?
2. Describe how teachers reacted to the presentation. What questions might have been posed to clarify the information?
3. Pretend that you are the building principal or special education director in this scenario. Tell how you would approach introducing RtI to the teachers. How would you encourage buy-in from teachers? How would your meeting or activities differ from the scenario presented in the case?

2

How to Implement Reading Assessment for Screening in the Elementary Classroom

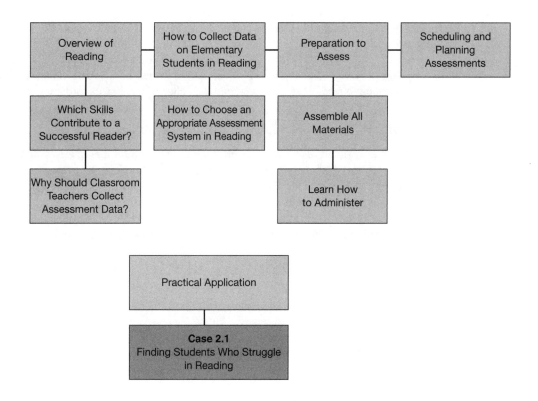

OVERVIEW OF READING

Which Skills Contribute to a Successful Reader?

It is important to understand the essential skills in reading when implementing the principles of RtI within the elementary classroom. The National Reading Panel was established by Congress in 1997 to identify important skills and principles essential in the teaching of reading. After this panel of experts methodically reviewed over 100,000 studies in reading, a report was issued in 2000 titled *Teaching Children to Read: An Evidence-Based Assessment of the Scientific Research Literature on Reading and Its Implications for Reading Instruction* (National Institute of Child Health and Human Development, 2000). This important report detailed five skills essential to reading instruction. One excellent source of usable, straightforward, and research-based information about these five essential skills (also called "Big Ideas in Reading") is available online from the University of Oregon (http://reading.uoregon.edu/). These essential skills of reading instruction are described in Table 2.1.

These essential skills of reading are connected on a developmental continuum beginning with early literacy (e.g., phonemes) to more advanced literacy (e.g., reading comprehension). To collect comprehensive data in reading, assessments use these five important skills in reading as a foundation. For example, it is believed that phonemic awareness is a strong predictor of student success in reading at the kindergarten and first-grade levels (National Institute of Child Health and Human Development, 2000). Therefore, it is useful to conduct screenings of all students in kindergarten and first grade on this skill at regular intervals to determine if any students are at risk for learning difficulty. Knowing who is at risk allows the teacher to confirm the existence of difficulty in learning to read, intervene early, and then closely monitor the progress of these students.

Why Should Classroom Teachers Collect Assessment Data?

Many of the assessments used to screen all students and monitor their progress in the elementary grades are focused on phonemic awareness, phonics, and fluency. The overarching questions for any classroom teacher include the following: Are students learning to read using the core curriculum? In other words, are they reaching established benchmarks in reading? If not, what can the teacher do? To structure answers to these questions, it is helpful to utilize ongoing systematic assessment within the three-tier model introduced in Chapter 1. This model is described in more detail in Table 2.2.

It is useful for elementary teachers to be knowledgeable of and plan to implement comprehensive assessment in these areas:

- Screening *all* students in the essential components of reading mentioned above in grade-appropriate areas three times per year (i.e., Tier 1)
- Monitoring the progress of *small groups* of students who require supplemental intervention (i.e., Tier 2) every other week
- Progress monitoring of *individual* students weekly for those requiring intensive intervention and instruction (i.e., Tier 3)

Although the general education teacher will likely be involved in progress monitoring for students at Tier 1 and Tier 2, at Tier 3 it is more typical for progress to be monitored by support professionals (e.g., a special education teacher or a literacy specialist).

Assessing students allows the classroom teacher to identify students who may not be able to meet benchmarks. Assessing students allows the classroom teacher to implement a quick

TABLE 2.1   Essential Skills of Reading

Phonemic Awareness

Definition	Ability to hear, identify, and use individual sounds in words
When is it assessed?	Typically assessed in kindergarten and first grade
Example	When asked what sounds are in the word *cat*, child says, "/k/ /a/ /t/"
Significance	Helps students learn to read and spell
Research suggested	Teaching phonemic awareness to children significantly improved their reading (National Institute of Child Health and Human Development, 2000)

Phonics

Definition	Ability to connect letters with sounds and to use sounds to form words; also called Alphabetic Principle (University of Oregon)
When is it assessed?	Usually assessed in mid-kindergarten through early second grade
Example	Student is able to read "words" like *sab, pid, wep*
Significance	Helps students connect letters with sounds and to decode unknown typical words
Research suggested	Systematic phonics instruction showed significant gains for students in kindergarten through sixth grade, including children experiencing difficulty learning to read (National Institute of Child Health and Human Development, 2000)

Fluency

Definition	Ability to read quickly and accurately connect words in a text
When is it assessed?	Usually assessed early first grade through sixth grade
Example	Student is able to read the following fluently: "John went to the store to buy apples and grapes. He walked quickly on the sidewalk." (More fluent readers spend energy on comprehension of the text; less fluent readers must focus energy on decoding individual words, impeding comprehension)
Significance	Reading fluency is considered an assessment of overall reading achievement (Fuchs et al., 2001; Wayman et al., 2007)
Research suggested	Guided oral reading is an effective way to improve fluency; silent reading doesn't appear to improve fluency (National Institute of Child Health and Human Development, 2000)

Vocabulary

Definition	Ability to understand words used to communicate
When is it assessed?	Not typically an area of assessment in elementary reading screening but is an important area for assessment, especially in middle and high schools
Example	In science class, students study how a microscope works and discuss the word, *microscope*. When reading the textbook, the student is able to decode the word *microscope* because he or she understands the vocabulary *microscope* and therefore fills in the word. Comprehension of the textbook is improved because the student understands the vocabulary.
Significance	If the student understands the meaning of a word, comprehension is enhanced
Research suggested	Vocabulary instruction should be taught both directly and indirectly; leads to improvement in comprehension; instruction must be developmentally appropriate (National Institute of Child Health and Human Development, 2000)

(continued)

TABLE 2.1   (continued)

Comprehension	
Definition	Ability to understand print in context; ability to gain meaning from text
When is it assessed?	Not typically an area of assessment in early elementary reading screening but is an important area for assessment throughout the upper grades
Example	Student is able to read a paragraph and understand the meaning of the text
Significance	The overall goal in reading is to comprehend
Research suggested	Comprehension can be improved by teaching specific cognitive strategies directly (National Institute of Child Health and Human Development, 2000)

response by providing supplemental intervention. The teacher can then track the progress of students receiving supplemental interventions. Consider this scenario as an analogy.

> *Imagine driving from Los Angeles to New York City to see a friend during the summer. To drive the most direct route, a map is used. The most direct route travels through Kansas City, St. Louis, and Columbus on the way to New York City. These points are benchmarks, and one anticipates staying on track by passing these benchmarks. Using a map, it is possible to reach the destination, New York City, using a direct route. If lost, the map, with its benchmarks, provides a way to get back on track.*
>
> *In a similar manner, a teacher walks into the classroom on the first day of school knowing the destination (i.e., all of students should learn to read and meet*

TABLE 2.2   Ongoing Systematic Assessment Model

Tier	Reading Focus/Group Size/Professionals Involved	Assessment Focus	Frequency of Assessment
Tier 1	Addresses five areas of reading in core reading program; large group; general education classroom teacher	Screen all children: Are at least 80% of students benefiting from instruction (i.e., meeting benchmarks)?	Three times/year: fall, winter, spring
Tier 2	Addresses focus of Tier 1 plus supplemental intervention in at least three of the five areas in reading; small group; general education classroom teacher; possibly involvement of a problem-solving team and/or support professionals (e.g., literacy specialist)	Monitor the progress of small groups of students	Every two weeks
Tier 3	Addresses focus of Tier 1 and Tier 2 plus intensive intervention (Tier 3) based on individual need; individualized instruction; general education teacher, problem-solving IEP team, and/or support professionals (e.g., special education teacher)	Monitor the progress of individual students	Weekly

Note: Students move between tiers based on their performance.
(*Sources:* Batsche et al., 2005; Kurns & Tilly, 2008; NASDSE, 2006; Pierangelo & Giuliani, 2008)

grade-appropriate reading standards). Use of a map (i.e., the core reading curriculum) guides the journey. In addition, the teacher will also track student progress to ensure that they reach the destination (i.e., learning to read) efficiently and are using the most direct route. The teacher certainly doesn't want to "get lost" on the way to the destination! If any students are "off track," the teacher implements research-based strategies and interventions to help the students get back "on track" to reaching the goal of learning to read.

By screening all students three times a year, the teacher can then deliver supplemental intervention before a student fails to learn to read. When small groups of students are identified through screening and confirmed with other assessment data to be in need of supplemental intervention, the teacher is able to monitor their progress more frequently (i.e., twice a month) to stay on track. Again, if these small groups are not on track (i.e., meeting benchmark expectations), then the instruction and/or interventions can be adjusted accordingly. Similarly, if individuals are not benefitting from the core instructional program with the addition of supplemental intervention, then they may need more intensive intervention, resulting in more frequent progress monitoring and assistance from specially trained personnel.

HOW TO COLLECT DATA ON ELEMENTARY STUDENTS IN READING

How to Choose an Appropriate Assessment System in Reading

There are a variety of tools to assess students in reading at various grade levels, and there are many useful plans for organizing assessment. All teachers should be informed of and knowledgeable about several assessment tools. Effective teachers carry around a toolbox, in much the same way as does a construction worker. In third grade, for example, an assessment tool in reading fluency is helpful in monitoring overall reading progress. There are multiple tools that could be used to assess one particular area in reading, and elementary teachers should have knowledge of and expertise in using several specific tools.

For this text, the focus of assessment in reading includes systematic universal screening of all students and progress monitoring of individual students who need supplementary or intensive intervention. Universal screening is characterized as

> a first stage within a screening process, to identify or predict students who may be at risk for poor learning outcomes. Universal screening assessments are typically brief; conducted with all students at a grade level; and followed by additional testing or short-term progress monitoring to corroborate students' risk status (American Institutes for Research, National Center on Response to Intervention, 2009, p. 5).

Progress monitoring "is used to assess students' academic performance, to quantify a student rate of improvement or responsiveness to instruction, and to evaluate the effectiveness of instruction. Progress monitoring can be implemented with individual students or an entire class" (American Institutes for Research, National Center on Response to Intervention, 2009, p. 3).

It is practical and efficient to use the same assessment system for both screening and progress monitoring, if feasible. In addition, assessments must be valid (i.e., the tool assesses what it intends to measure), reliable (i.e., the tool measures consistently across time and evaluator), sensitive to student growth (i.e., the tool uses data for progress monitoring), and accurate in identifying students who need supplemental intervention (for screening). Table 2.3 summarizes several commonly used lower cost assessments for screening and progress monitoring.

TABLE 2.3 Screening Instruments and Progress Monitoring Instruments

Specific Assessment	Purpose	Is It Accurate (Screening Instrument) and/or Sensitive (Progress Monitoring Instrument)?	Is It Valid?	Is It Reliable?	Approximate Start-Up Cost for First Year (Based on A Classroom of 25 Students)
AIMSweb— Early literacy (beginning sounds, letter names, letter sounds, phonemic segmentation, nonsense words), oral reading fluency, reading comprehension (Reading Maze)	Screening and progress monitoring	Partially convincing evidence	Yes	Yes	$125
Dynamic Indicators of Basic Early Literacy Skills (DIBELS)—letter-naming fluency, nonsense word fluency, oral reading fluency, phoneme segmentation fluency	Screening and progress monitoring	Range from partially convincing evidence to unconvincing (phonemic segmentation fluency, letter naming fluency)	Yes, for all except phoneme segmentation fluency (partially convincing evidence)	Range from partially convincing evidence to unconvincing evidence (phonemic segmentation fluency)	$73 if prepared materials and scoring system are purchased; all materials can be downloaded for free from the DIBELS Web site (materials must then be copied)
STEEP (System to Enhance Educational Performance)—oral reading fluency	Screening and progress monitoring	Convincing evidence	Yes	Partially convincing evidence	$38 (must have Internet access to implement)
Curriculum-based measurement in reading (CBM-R)—letter-sound fluency, maze fluency, passage-reading fluency, word identification fluency	Progress monitoring	Yes	Yes	Yes	$40
Teacher-constructed curriculum-based measurement probes— oral reading fluency		Yes, if standard instructions and procedures are followed			

(*Source*: Information from American Institutes for Research, National Center on Response to Intervention, 2009)

Many screening and progress-monitoring assessment instruments are based on curriculum-based measurement (CBM). CBM assessments are much like mini-achievement tests. They typically use initial sound fluency, phonemic awareness, and letter-recognition probes at the early literacy levels and oral reading-fluency probes for older students or after students master early reading skills. CBM uses brief probes to assess students in reading, and results can be easily summarized. CBM is well-supported by research as valid, reliable, and sensitive to student growth (Wayman et al., 2007).

For this text, two exemplary assessment tools are detailed in the appendices. Appendix A describes how to prepare and administer teacher-constructed, curriculum-based oral-reading fluency probes (appropriate for progress monitoring from Grade1 and above). Appendix B describes preparation and administration instructions for Dynamic Indicators of Basic Early Literacy Skills (DIBELS; University of Oregon) assessments (appropriate for screening and progress monitoring from kindergarten and above). After reading this chapter, the reader may want to determine if either example detailed in the appendices is appropriate and then select one or both of these assessment systems for implementation.

Other options for screening and progress monitoring could also be reviewed (see Table 2.3). For example, AIMSweb is a comprehensive assessment system used for screening and progress monitoring. One unique feature about AIMSweb is that it includes comprehension assessment, the Reading Maze. When administering the Reading Maze, students are asked to silently read a graded reading selection. The first sentence is left intact. After the first sentence, every seventh word is replaced by three word choices in parenthesis. One of the three words is correct, and the student must circle the correct choice.

Research suggests that reading fluency might be the best measure for primary students (after mastery of early reading skills) and that maze assessment might be most appropriate for intermediate and secondary students (Wayman et al., 2007). In selecting an appropriate assessment system, the following questions are useful:

1. What is the purpose of the assessment? Is the purpose universal screening? It the purpose progress monitoring? Is the purpose to further define strengths and weaknesses (i.e., diagnosis)? It is essential to select an instrument that fits the purpose of the assessment. For example, if the assessment is to be used for universal screening, then it does not need to be sensitive to student growth. However, if the purpose of assessment is to monitor the progress of a small group of kindergarten students who did not meet the reading benchmarks, then the assessment must be sensitive to student growth. DIBELS uses phonemic segmentation fluency and initial sound fluency to monitor progress in kindergarten reading and is sensitive to student growth. Therefore, this instrument would be appropriate. Conversely, it is likely that a standardized group assessment of reading skills would not be sensitive to student growth and would continue to be appropriate.

2. Does the grade level match the parameters of the assessment? The assessment must be appropriate for the grade level assessed. For example, because phonemic awareness is an important early foundational skill in reading, a screening assessment system for kindergarten students would include this skill. Conversely, oral reading fluency would not be an appropriate screening instrument for kindergarten because this age level of students doesn't typically develop oral-reading fluency skills until they master early reading skills like phonemic awareness.

3. What resources are available? All assessments involve some monetary resources. Some require access to the Internet and a copy machine so that materials can be downloaded and copied. Others require monetary commitment to purchase the supplies. It is also useful to assess human resources available. For example, if a paraprofessional is available to assist in preparing materials, the time needed to prepare decreases.

4. How much advance planning time is needed to organize and prepare the assessment? Teachers cannot adequately prepare assessments for screening and progress monitoring unless advance planning occurs. It is important to estimate the amount of time needed to prepare, organize, and learn to administer assessments and plan ahead. Sometimes breaks in the school year offer natural pauses in teaching to prepare assessments.

PREPARATION TO ASSESS

After selection of the assessment system(s), the teacher must learn to administer assessments, score assessments, prepare materials, practice assessing, develop a workable assessment schedule, analyze assessment data, and summarize the results. Table 2.4 summarizes timelines for screening and progress monitoring.

As discussed in Chapter 1, the intent of screening is to determine the extent to which students are learning to read using the core curriculum and to identify any students who do not meet reading benchmarks. For students who do not meet benchmarks, it is essential to confirm this assumption with at least one additional assessment. For example, if one first-grade student did not meet the benchmarks for nonsense word fluency and phonics, it would be important to confirm that these scores really reflected the student's performance. It is possible that the student wasn't feeling well during the screening and the scores didn't reflect the student's performance. Therefore, at least one other source of assessment data confirming the existence of a real difficulty in reading would be necessary. This assessment confirmation could include progress monitoring for 6 weeks, a standardized assessment (e.g., core reading curriculum tests), or other appropriate assessment data. Screening, with appropriate confirmation, will assist the teacher in determining which tier (1, 2, or 3) the student is performing at and help in knowing when to systematically apply interventions. Progress monitoring (the focus of Chapter 4) is essential in tracking the progress of students identified for supplemental intervention in Tier 2 and applying more intensive intervention in Tier 3.

The remainder of this chapter assumes that an appropriate assessment instrument has been selected. Steps to prepare, organize, and learn to administer assessments are addressed.

Assemble All Materials

Step 1: Print (or purchase) all assessment materials. Assessment materials typically include the following:
- Student response materials (materials the student reads)
- teacher recording and scoring materials (materials the teacher uses to record, score, and summarize student responses)

TABLE 2.4   Timelines for Screening and Progress Monitoring

Purpose	Schedule
Screening	Fall screening (August–November)
	Winter screening (December–February)
	Spring screening (March–May)
Progress monitoring	Every 2 weeks for small groups receiving supplementary intervention (i.e., Tier 2)
	Weekly for individuals receiving intensive intervention (i.e., Tier 3)

- An administration and scoring manual (used by the teacher to learn how to administer the assessment and accurately score student results)

Step 2: Copy, assemble, and organize materials. Many assessment instruments require *one* copy of the student response material for all students in the classroom (to be used over and over again) and *one* copy of the administration and scoring manual. Typically, assessment instruments require *multiple* teacher scoring and recording materials (one for each student in the classroom). Organize the materials by separating the materials into three categories: student materials, teacher materials, and administration and scoring manuals. It might be useful to place the student reusable stimulus materials in a notebook and label it. If the assessment instrument includes both screening and progress-monitoring tools, make sure these are separated and labeled.

Learn How to Administer

Step 3: Thoroughly read the administration and scoring guide. It is essential to thoroughly understand how to administer the assessment. Sometimes there are longer, more detailed instructions in the administration manual and short-form directions within the teacher scoring materials. It is very important to read and understand both.

Step 4: Find an adult partner (preferably someone who is familiar with assessment, such as another teacher, school psychologist, or speech therapist) who is willing to play the part of a student. Practice administering the screening assessments, and then the progress-monitoring assessments, paying special attention to following the procedures and directions *exactly* as they are stated. Practice at least 10 times or until completely comfortable administering all assessments.

Step 5: Practice administrating the assessment to a child in a classroom with an observer taking notes. The observing partner should make sure that the instrument is administered *exactly* as intended. Some assessments include a specific Assessment Integrity Checklist (e.g., AIMSweb, DIBELS) to use as the teacher administers an assessment. If a checklist is not included, Table 2.5 might be useful to ensure that the assessment is administered as intended. As the teacher administers an assessment, the observing partner checks each item to indicate if the teacher is proficient or needs additional practice with the assessment. After each assessment, the partner should review this completed checklist with the teacher. If additional practice is needed, steps 4 and 5 should be repeated until all items on the checklist are listed as proficient.

SCHEDULING AND PLANNING ASSESSMENTS

After assembling the materials and learning to administer the assessment, the teacher is now ready to begin scheduling assessments. With advance planning, a teacher should be able to assess each student in the class three times per year for screening purposes and, for those who need supplementary or intensive intervention, monitor progress more frequently. There are many ways to schedule screening and progress-monitoring assessments. The most important points are to plan ahead, be consistent, and build regular assessment time into the schedule. Assessment must be a high-priority activity. To illustrate how important scheduling should be, consider this analogy.

As a dog owner, Jamil recognizes that his dog needs to be walked outside several times per day. Typically, he knows when his dog needs to be walked, and he builds

TABLE 2.5 **Appropriate Assessment Administration Checklist: Informal Observation by an Adult Partner**

Examiner_____   Date_____

Observer_____   Name of Assessment_____

Directions: Check the appropriate response as the examiner administers the assessment.

Procedure to Observe	Yes, Performed Correctly	No, Did Not Perform Correctly, Needs Additional Practice
1. Arranged teacher scoring materials so that the child could not view the materials.	Yes	No
2. Arranged the assessment environment to minimize distractions.	Yes	No
3. All necessary materials were present.	Yes	No
4. Assessment procedures were adequately explained.	Yes	No
5. Rapport was established before beginning the assessment.	Yes	No
6. Read standard directions verbatim.	Yes	No
7. Avoided distracting mannerisms.	Yes	No
8. Gave student ample and appropriate encouragement and support.	Yes	No
9. Spoke at appropriate volume for the setting.	Yes	No
10. Manipulated materials with ease and confidence.	Yes	No
11. Used vocabulary suited to the student's age.	Yes	No
12. Praised child appropriately (e.g., did not praise correct answers but praised effort).	Yes	No
13. Paced assessment to suit child's ability.	Yes	No
14. Accurately recorded responses in the record book (i.e., responded to accurate and inaccurate responses as detailed in the teacher scoring manual).	Yes	No
15. Scored the assessment accurately.	Yes	No

*this time into his schedule. This dog-walking becomes routine, and Jamil's dog even knows when it is time to go out, running to the door and wagging her tail. Even in bad weather, Jamil walks the dog. If he is out of town, Jamil makes arrangements for someone else to walk his dog. In fact, Jamil probably wouldn't think of **not** walking his dog, even if he were tired or busy. Walking his dog is just part of the daily routine and responsible pet ownership.*

    This simple analogy applies the same logic a teacher should use when scheduling assessment time. The teacher understands that students will benefit from assessment, and the assessment becomes routine. The teacher considers assessment an important part of instruction and an important responsibility to students.

    The following are useful steps in scheduling assessment time for screening and progress monitoring.

Step 1: Plan a regular time each week to assess students and analyze data, marking this time on a calendar. Estimate about 5 minutes per student for screening or progress monitoring.

Step 2: During this time, it will be important to plan meaningful independent work for students while the teacher conducts individual assessments. To successfully plan and

TABLE 2.6   Guiding Principles: Instructional Management for Independent Practice

Planning	Activities must be relevant to what is taught.
	Activities should enhance what has already been taught (should not be introduce a new skill). Skills already learned can be repeated, applied, or extended.
	Students should be able to succeed with the assigned work. Activities should not be too easy or too difficult.
	All materials and space should be organized in advance.
Implementation	Independent-activity procedures should be taught and then practiced in the same manner as any subject matter. Procedures should be reviewed periodically. When teaching, use verbal descriptions, examples/non-examples, and modeling.
	Outcome (product) of the activity should be promptly reinforced after completion.

Guiding Principles: Behavioral Management for Independent Practice

Planning	Develop a small number (3–4) of independent-practice rules that are consistent with school policy.
	Rules should be stated objectively (e.g., "Say please and thank you," not "Be polite").
	Rules should be stated positively (tell students what they *should* do, not what they are *not* supposed to do).
	Rules should include specific consequences for violations.
	Rules should be displayed visually and prominently in the classroom.
	Anticipate potential problems with following rules and develop a contingency plan (e.g., student asks for help with an independent activity and the teacher is conducting an assessment).
Implementation	Rules should be taught and then practiced in the same manner as any subject matter. Rules should be reviewed periodically. When teaching, use verbal descriptions, examples/non-examples, and modeling.
	Rules and expectations should be clearly communicated.
	Teacher response to rule violation should be consistent and matter-of-fact. If a rule violation occurs, verbally repeat the rule. If the violation continues, apply the consequence.
	At the end of independent-practice/assessment time, praise students who followed rules and procedures. Catch students who display good behavior (e.g., "Thank you for working so quietly," "I like the way you finished this assignment").

(*Source:* Information from Mastropieri & Scruggs, 2007)

implement independent work for the majority of the class, behavioral and instructional management become important. Table 2.6 provides several useful guiding principles.

Examples of independent activities could include reading learning stations, individual seatwork to practice a skill, reading orally to a partner, and use of technology to reinforce reading. The time should be well planned and consistent for students and should involve meaningful activities. Please note that it is essential to maintain a regular schedule throughout the school year. This scheduled time will allow the teacher to be able to screen students, monitor student progress (discussed in Chapter 4), and provide small-group instruction and interventions (discussed in Chapter 3).

Step 3: Arrange space in the classroom to conduct assessments. For assessment space, a semiprivate, relatively quiet space with a table and two chairs will be needed where one student can read aloud. In addition, access to a clock with a second hand or a stopwatch will be needed.

TABLE 2.7   Screening Schedule Example

Day 1 (2:30 pm–3:00 pm) Monday	Day 2 (2:30 pm–3:00 pm) Tuesday	Day 3 (2:30 pm–3:00 pm) Wednesday	Day 4 (2:30 pm–3:00 pm) Thursday	Day 5 (2:30 pm–3:00 pm) Friday
John	Pam	Beth	James	Curtis
Tamisha	Libby	Jean	Devon	Fran
Mary	Phil	Sam	Anthony	Anna
Rowena	Mario	Mark	Sun Yu	Patty
George	Sherry	Joey	Lakisha	Rowena

Step 4: Decide who will be assessed each week during the screening period. If screening an entire class of 25 students in first grade, for example, it would be feasible to assess 5 students each day beginning in September. The screening schedule might look like Table 2.7.

After screening during this week, this scheduled time would be used to implement progress monitoring, summarize and analyze assessment data, and/or to provide supplementary intervention during subsequent weeks.

Step 5: The assessment plan should be introduced to students and to their parents. For example, one fifth-grade teacher discussed with parents the following at the beginning of the yearly orientation meeting:

> *I am planning to monitor the progress of some students in reading this year, with the goal of providing early intervention should any child need an extra boost in reading. I typically assess each child in reading throughout the year, but this year, I am implementing an additional system of assessment. At least once every two weeks, and sometimes weekly, I will give the students a short assessment that involves reading aloud for 1 minute. This may not seem like a good assessment, but research indicates that these types of brief assessments can indicate student progress over time. This simple assessment, combined with my other assessments, will help me understand how well selected students are meeting overall reading expectations. I will incorporate this new assessment into our normal classroom routine. Each student will be taught to graph his or her own progress. These graphs will be shared with parents at parent conferences in November. I want to share an example of these graphs with you today.*

Students also need a similar introduction to the assessments, including what the assessment involves and how it will be incorporated into the daily routine. As indicated in the example above, students could also be taught to understand, graph, and monitor their progress over time. If students are asked to graph their individual assessment results, they will need to be directly taught how to use a graph, plot the results, and understand their meaning. It is important for parents and students to understand the assessment process.

Step 6: Assess individual students.

Chapter 3 addresses how to summarize and make decisions based on screening assessment data and how to address student needs based on the data.

PRACTICAL APPLICATION

CASE 2.1

Finding Students Who Struggle in Reading

After teaching third grade for 5 years in a school where I am the only third-grade teacher, I consider myself an optimist. I am optimistic that my students, given time and patience on my part, will perform up to the expectations for third-grade students in our school and state. In the past, when I noticed that students began to struggle, I pulled them aside and gave them individual attention and extra support. For example, I remember one student, Carlos. Carlos experienced considerable difficulty with phonics, and he struggled to identify words and read fluently. I worked individually several times a week with Carlos by providing extra phonics activities. By the end of the year, I felt that Carlos had made good progress in reading. In fourth grade, Carlos did well in reading. However, more recently, two other students struggled in my class, even though they seemed to be progressing. How could I have overlooked their difficulties?

I have a good working relationship with other teachers in my building and meet periodically with the kindergarten, first-, second-, and fourth-grade teachers to discuss curriculum issues. Last year, we noticed that six students were referred for special education in fourth grade. After some discussion, we came to the conclusion that students experience more academic difficulty in fourth grade because the material is more challenging. The early grades focus more on concrete activities that make learning fun. In fourth grade, the expectations change to more formal learning with significantly higher expectations. After analyzing why we thought these students were referred for special education, my colleagues and I didn't feel that changes needed to be made in the curriculum. We just assumed that these six students could not have been identified earlier as needing special assistance. However, I am beginning to question the accuracy of our assumption. Could we have identified them before they failed?

This year, I decided to try some of the techniques associated with the Response to Intervention process. I attended several workshops on how to administer screening and progress-monitoring assessments in reading to students in my class. I was paired up with a speech pathologist to practice administering the assessments and was able to prepare all assessment materials for the upcoming school year. In October, I began screening my students using the DIBELS reading protocol. I predicted that the results would show that two of my students, James and Chancellor, would not meet expectations. These two boys displayed difficulty reading fluently and sounding out words.

After administering the screening, I summarized my students' scores on a chart. The scoring guidelines indicated that students who read between 0 and 70 words per minute were *at risk* for developing difficulty in reading, those who read between 71 and 92 words per minute were at *some risk*, and those who read 93 or more words per minute were at *low risk* in developing difficulty in reading.

When reviewing the results, to my surprise, five students did not meet the expected benchmarks for third grade. Wow! I was shocked, because I generally have a good sense of who in my classroom struggles with reading. The other three students, Juanita, Amy, and Carlos, were quiet, well behaved, and cooperative students in class, but their performance on the screening assessment indicated that they were at risk for experiencing difficulty in reading.

Based solely on the screening results, I implemented a research-based intervention for these five students in reading. After about 6 weeks, I could see that each student was improving.

I feel that this new process helped me identify students who were at risk of having difficulty in reading. If I had not screened the students in my class, I would have missed several students who needed extra help in reading. I wonder if these students would have been referred for special education in fourth grade.

TABLE A: CASE 2.1   Oral Reading Fluency

Screening: Fall (October 15–19)

Name	Low Risk	Some Risk	High Risk
James	93	75	
Bill	95		
Mary	101		
Elizabeth	182		
Juanita		89	
Amy		84	
John	98		
Anna	117		
Pat	101		
Chancellor		78	
Joe	111		
Cortez	129		
Will	99		
Chris	94		
Andrew	99		
Elise	151		
Jordan	96		
Shawna	103		
Carlos	110		58
Latrice	104		
Nahid	120		

Scores: Number of words read correctly in 1 minute.

I like this new screening process because I can administer the assessments quickly to my whole class without involving the whole school, and I can discover students at risk of developing reading difficulty in my class and hopefully avoid referral to special education in fourth grade. I can easily provide additional time in the core curriculum and supplemental intervention without help from outside resources.

Questions

1. Why do you think this teacher's initial prediction about who was experiencing difficulty in reading was incorrect?
2. How do these assessment results relate to the issue of special education referral discussed at the beginning of the case?
3. How does implementation of the principles of RtI address teachers' assumptions about why students perform poorly in later years?
4. Describe how you think this teacher prepared to administer the assessments. Include best practice in your description.
5. After screening all students, what step did this teacher miss? Why is this step important?
6. What do you think will happen next? What should happen if any of the five students don't make progress?

3

How to Make Decisions and Meet Student Needs Based on Assessment Data

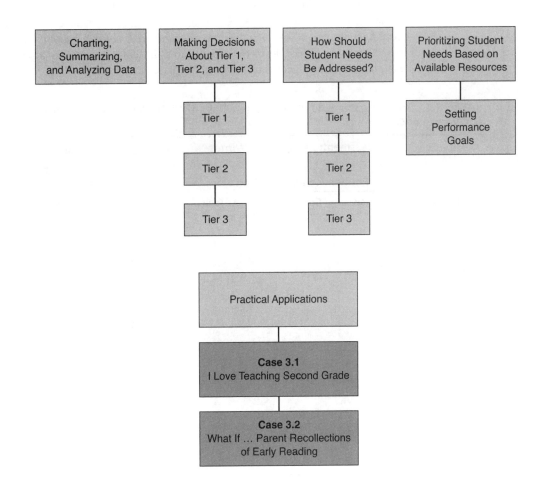

CHARTING, SUMMARIZING, AND ANALYZING DATA

Individual student assessment data must be summarized and analyzed to make appropriate decisions about instruction. Many assessment systems provide useful summary charts so that classroom teachers can make appropriate decisions about results. Often, there is a fee associated with use of commercial assessment systems. However, assuming that the individual teacher has few resources, data can be analyzed using the following steps.

Step 1: Construct a class summary chart. After screening students in reading, the teacher should summarize scores on a summary chart. As an example, in February, a kindergarten teacher with 19 students administered two screening assessments using DIBELS (University of Oregon), phonemic segmentation fluency, and nonsense word fluency. First, each child's score is computed after assessing by adding the number of correct responses. Then individual scores are recorded on a class summary chart. For DIBELS, the instruction manual provides interpretation on how many correct responses each student needs to be "low risk," "some risk," or "high risk" for experiencing difficulty in reading. For example, a student who scored between 0 and 6 on phonemic segmentation fluency is considered "at risk." If a student scores 18 or above on this assessment, the student is considered "low risk." On the summary chart, student scores are grouped according to the extent to which they meet benchmarks. The chart summarizes which students are at which risk level for experiencing difficulty in a particular area. Table 3.1 summarizes student scores from this kindergarten class.

TABLE 3.1   Screening Example: Kindergarten Class of 19 Students Using DIBELS (University of Oregon)

| | Assessment: Fall_____ Winter_____ X_____ Spring_____ | | | | | |
| | Score: Phonemic Segmentation | | | Score: Nonsense Word Fluency | | |
Student	Low Risk	Some Risk	At Risk	Low Risk	Some Risk	At Risk
John	20			14		
Tim	26			17		
Shawna	25			13		
Terrence	28			22		
Asiah	27			25		
Aijaz	30			28		
Logan	26			24		
Shefali	19			15		
Kayla	27			25		
Aaron	18			16		
Taylor	18			13		
Devan	21			15		
Adrian	24			20		
Jose	22			16		
Karisa	23			17		
Supriya	25			22		
Carolita		8			7	
Mary		11			11	
Paul			4			2

TABLE 3.2   **Examples of Additional Assessments in Reading**

Additional Assessment Procedure	Description	Grade Levels
Monitor student progress over a period of 6 weeks.	Use a progress-monitoring tool (e.g., CBM, DIBELS), check the progress of the student every other week over a period of 6 weeks to confirm that the student experiences continued difficulty in reading.	Elementary
Classroom Reading Inventory (10th ed.) (Silvaroli & Wheelock, 2004); Informal Reading Inventory (7th ed.) (Roe & Burns, 2007)	The student reads graded word lists and/or reading selections orally. The examiner can determine the level at which the student reads, conduct error and miscue analysis, and determine the level of comprehension.	Elementary
BRIGANCE Diagnostic Comprehensive Inventory of Basic Skills–Revised (Brigance, 1999)	A criterion-referenced assessment addressing oral reading, comprehension, word analysis, and functional word recognition	Prekindergarten–grade 9
Teacher observation of instructional environment (McLoughlin & Lewis, 2008)	Teacher observation of level at which the student reads comfortably via informal observation of reading errors, etc.	Elementary
Running Records (Clay, 2000)	The student reads a selection aloud while the teacher counts number of words read correctly and records errors.	Elementary
Other teacher-constructed curriculum-based assessments (http://www. interventioncentral.com/tools.php)	The student reads common sight words, orally identifies letters of the alphabet, and orally reads text.	Elementary
Other informal assessments	Parent interview, report card grades, observed reading skill in content area subjects	Elementary

Notice that 16 students are categorized "low risk," 2 students are "some risk," and 1 student is "at risk" in both of these assessments.

Step 2: Confirm with at least one additional assessment any students who are categorized as "some risk" or "at risk." The results of one single assessment should not be used as the sole determination of a student's academic or behavioral functioning. Other assessment data could include formal assessment (standardized or norm referenced) or informal assessment (non-norm referenced). Examples of typical formal and informal assessments in reading are included in Table 3.2.

As an example, consider the following scenario.

Mr. Liu administered the AIMSweb Maze screening assessment in reading to all students in his fourth-grade class. The assessment consisted of each student silently reading a fourth-grade reading selection. Every seventh word was replaced by a choice of three words, and the student had to circle the word that made sense. The Benchmark Teacher Report ranked students according to their overall performance in comprehension, from "above average" to "average" to "below average" to "well below average." Out of 20 students, June was "below average" and Bradley was categorized "well below average. Mr. Liu was able to confirm that Bradley really was func-

tioning well below average by reviewing additional assessment data. Bradley was receiving assistance from the Title I reading instructor twice a week, and a review of his records showed that reading grades from kindergarten through third grade were unsatisfactory. In addition, Bradley's mother previously contacted Mr. Liu to express concerns about Bradley's confidence in completing homework. Mr. Liu also noticed that Bradley struggled with word recognition when reading aloud. Assessment data for the other student, June, did not confirm existence of "below average" functioning in reading. Mr. Liu observed that June read successfully in class during social studies and science. She also worked in an independent reading program on the computer, and the program indicated that June easily comprehended grade-level materials. Mr. Liu concluded that the screening results did not accurately reflect June's reading skill level and that she appeared to be progressing well despite her performance on the screening. June continued to participate in regular reading screening with other students during the school year.

MAKING DECISIONS ABOUT TIER 1, TIER 2, AND TIER 3

Tier 1

At Tier 1, it is expected that the majority of students, approximately 80%, will meet reading benchmarks based on the screening assessment (Batsche et al., 2005). This can be considered an important factor in determining if the core curriculum is appropriate. Most students typically respond to the core curriculum in reading. If fewer than approximately 80% of students meet the reading benchmarks, this could mean that they are not responding adequately to the core curriculum. If the core curriculum meets the needs of fewer than 80% of students, the core curriculum should be reviewed before assuming that many students need supplementary instruction. Several guiding questions may lead to more specific definition of why students are not responding to the core curriculum. These questions help in reviewing the core curriculum and determining how it fits with other grade levels in reading.

1. To what extent is the core curriculum aligned with state-approved grade-level standards? If it is not aligned, then the lack of performance at the expected level could be due to expectations being set too high by the school as compared to state standards.
2. Does the core curriculum include extensive and explicit vocabulary instruction, especially for English language learners (Gersten et al., 2007)? If not, is vocabulary systematically taught as part of the curriculum?
3. Is there a common curriculum used from grade to grade? If not, the core curriculum is probably not aligned with the standards, resulting in fragmented instruction from grade to grade.
4. To what extent are teachers across grade levels and within the same grade level following the core curriculum? If they are not following the core curriculum (assuming the core is aligned with state standards), then expectations could be adversely affected.
5. Are key reading skills addressed at the developmentally appropriate time of year with the correct emphasis? Again, if the core curriculum is aligned with state standards, this would not become an issue.
6. Are support systems in place to assist teachers in utilizing effective teaching strategies? Lesson plans could be aligned with the core curriculum, and the core could be aligned with state standards, but if the teacher does not use effective strategies, the student may not perform at expected levels.

7. Do teachers operationalize the belief that all children can learn to read by differentiating instruction? Teachers may say that they believe that all students can learn, but if they do not differentiate their instruction, then students may not perform at expected levels.

8. After reviewing reading lesson plans and the instructional approaches used to teach reading, is the teaching consistent with the core curriculum instructions? If so, discrepancies are probably due to student performance.

Based on how the problem is defined and the factors that contribute to the discrepancy in assessment data, the teacher will formulate a plan to ensure that instruction aligns with the core curriculum or further investigate the core curriculum. For example, if the first-grade teacher uses the core curriculum, the second-grade teacher uses phonics instruction from various sources, and the third-grade teacher teaches the reading of novels as the primary curriculum, it seems apparent that there is little consistency on skill development from grade to grade. This inconsistency would frame the changes that need to occur. The issue of core curriculum effectiveness cannot be ignored (Kurns & Tilly, 2008). If data suggest that many students are not responding to the core curriculum, extensive supplemental intervention cannot meet the needs of all children nor take the place of the core curriculum for all children. Because the core curriculum affects the majority of students, it is most efficient to first address the factors that affect the majority of students before designing and implementing supplemental or intensive intervention that might affect fewer students, even though this intervention is important.

A core reading curriculum should be appropriate for the developmental level of students, evidence based, address the important areas of reading, and be aligned with state standards. For information in evaluating the core reading curriculum (K–3) and reviews of several programs in reading, the following resource may be useful: *The Consumer's Guide to Evaluating a Core Reading Program* (http://reading.uoregon.edu/cia/curricula/index.php). Using this guide, a teacher could evaluate a core reading program for kindergarten, first, second, or third grade by determining if the program is efficient and analyzing critical elements of reading within the program.

Tier 2

Batsche et al. (2005) suggested that approximately 10% to 15% of students in a given class are at some risk for experiencing academic difficulty. To determine how to identify a student at Tier 2, the following procedure could be implemented after screening results show that the student did not reach the established reading benchmarks.

- For students who do not meet screening benchmarks, confirm with at least one other assessment that these scores really reflect the students' functioning (as stated earlier in this chapter). One practical way to confirm screening results is to monitor the progress of these students for 6 weeks. If, after 6 weeks, a student still does not meet the reading benchmarks, the student should be provided with systematic, research-based supplemental intervention. There are many different assessments that could verify the existence of difficulty in reading, and monitoring progress for 6 weeks is just one.

Supplemental interventions are addressed later in this chapter. In addition, progress should be monitored (as described in Chapter 4) at least every other week.

Tier 3

Students at Tier 3 represent a very small number of students who do not respond to the core curriculum or to supplemental intervention. These students need intensive, individualized intervention. Batsche et al. (2005) suggested that approximately 5% of students in a class function at Tier 3. For a student to be considered at Tier 3, the procedure listed above for Tier 2 should be followed. If, after 6 to 8 weeks of supplemental intervention, the student still does not meet established reading benchmarks, the student should be considered for Tier 3, or intensive, intervention. At this point, it is appropriate to consult with the building-based intervention team to plan individually for services or to consider a referral for additional assistance. This referral could include special education.

HOW SHOULD STUDENT NEEDS BE ADDRESSED?

Tier 1

If about 80% of the students are meeting reading benchmarks as assessed in screening, students are responding to the core curriculum. In this case, the core curriculum is meeting the majority of students' needs, and the teacher will continue implementing the core curriculum for this group and all students. Teachers typically devote between 75 and 90 minutes per day to core reading instruction. They will also continue regular screening three times per year.

It might be helpful for the teacher to self-assess instruction to make certain that he or she is addressing the needs of the entire class using the core reading program. Table 3.3 is a self-assessment that could be completed following reading instruction for elementary students. This assessment was adapted from *Principal Reading Walk-through Checklists* (Florida Center for Reading Research, n.d.).

Other Issues:
- Was the objective developmentally appropriate for your grade-level standards?
- How were students grouped? (large group, small group, individual)
- To what extent were students engaged in the lesson? (most students engaged, some engaged, few engaged)
- Was vocabulary taught explicitly and directly, especially for English language learners (Gersten et al., 2007)?

Reflection:
- In what areas was your answer no?
- What will you do differently during the next reading lesson?

Tier 2

For all students who do not meet benchmarks on the screening assessment and where at least one additional assessment confirms the screening results, systematic supplementary research-based intervention should be provided. In addition, the teacher will continue to provide instruction using the core curriculum, in the same manner as with other students who are meeting expectations (Tier 1). The supplementary intervention would be in addition to the daily core instruction.

If implemented systematically and with intensity, this action is likely to result in student improvement. There is strong research evidence to support systematic implementation of supplemental intervention for small groups (Gersten et al., 2009), including English language learners (Gersten et al., 2007). These steps could be followed in implementing supplementary intervention.

BEFORE THE SCHOOL YEAR BEGINS

Step 1: Review potential supplementary reading programs that are evidence based and that address up to four important areas of reading (e.g., phonemic awareness, phonics, fluency, vocabulary, comprehension). This step should ideally occur well in advance of

TABLE 3.3   Self-Assessment of Reading Instruction, Elementary

Instructional Issue	*Yes:* I planned this component in advance; I fully understood this component; I completely carried out this component in the lesson.	*Partially:* I thought about this component in advance but didn't specifically plan to implement the component; I partially understood this component; I partially carried out this component in the lesson or carried it out incidentally.	*No:* I did not consider this component in advance; I have little/no understanding of this component; I did not carry out this component in the lesson.
Was the learning objective for the lesson clearly communicated to students?			
Did the behavior management system create a positive atmosphere for learning?			
Was the physical arrangement of the classroom conducive to large-group instruction and small-group instruction?			
Were at least 75–90 minutes devoted to reading instruction?			
Was additional time scheduled for reading assessment and supplementary intervention?			
Were your interactions with students warm, encouraging, and enthusiastic?			
Did you convey the perception that all students can learn to read?			
Were all reading materials organized and easily accessible?			
Did you use several different materials during instruction to support student learning?			

(continued)

TABLE 3.3 (Continued)

Instructional Issue	*Yes:* I planned this component in advance; I fully understood this component; I completely carried out this component in the lesson.	*Partially:* I thought about this component in advance but didn't specifically plan to implement the component; I partially understood this component; I partially carried out this component in the lesson or carried it out incidentally.	*No:* I did not consider this component in advance; I have little/no understanding of this component; I did not carry out this component in the lesson.
Was instruction clear and explicit?			
Did you implement the core reading program as intended?			
Did you differentiate instruction to meet the needs of all students?			
Were there ample opportunities for student practice?			
Did you give clear, positive feedback frequently to students?			
Was your instruction paced to meet student needs?			
Did students understand routines and procedures?			
Did you try to motivate students?			
Did you have clearly designed and labeled reading centers or activities during independent work time?			
Were students actively engaged during independent work time?			
Did you address these important areas of reading instruction: Phonics, Vocabulary, Fluency, Comprehension?			

(Adapted from *Principal Reading Walk-through Checklists*, by Florida Center for Reading Research, n.d. Retrieved April 15, 2009, from http://www.fcrr.org/Curriculum/curriculum.htm)

the school year, because it is essential to be informed, well planned, and organized. A supplemental reading activity or program should be one that research indicates is highly likely to achieve results. There are several sources to help teachers select appropriate evidence-based supplementary reading programs and/or activities. Several of these resources are listed and described below.

- *What Works Clearinghouse*, U.S. Department of Education (http://ies.ed.gov/ncee/wwc/reports/) At this site, specific programs are listed in early reading and are rated according to an improvement index (to what extent the program made a difference in reading achievement), evidence rating (quality of research design used to investigate the program), and extent of evidence (amount of evidence used to determine the rating).
- *Florida Center for Reading Research* (http://www.fcrr.org/FCRRReports/CReportsCS.aspx?rep=supp) At this site, several reading programs are evaluated.
- *Intervention Central* (http://www.interventioncentral.com) This site describes a wealth of classroom activities and interventions in reading fluency and comprehension, along with many other content-specific activities and general classroom activities.
- *Free Reading* (http://www.free-reading.net) Included in this resource are specific activities in the areas of phonological awareness, phonics, comprehension, vocabulary, fluency, and writing.

Kerns and Tilly (2008) suggested using the following continuum when deciding which programs are supported by research. First, look for research-validated materials where practices and materials are supported by research, then look for research-validated practices where practices have been supported by research but materials may not have been researched. Last, look for materials that are designed based on important fundamentals of effective instruction.

Step 2: Select several supplementary interventions and learn to implement them with integrity. Integrity means that the program should be used in the manner in which it was intended. Integrity could be achieved by practice, observing another professional using the program, and/or attending professional development activities to learn how to implement the intervention as intended. This step should ideally occur well in advance of the school year, just like Step 1, because identified programs may need to be purchased and time spent in learning how to implement the program(s).

Step 3: Organize materials for implementation. Make sure that materials are ready and accessible for use. This may include copying, storing, and/or labeling materials for easy access.

DURING THE SCHOOL YEAR

Step 1: After conducting the first reading screening, summarize student assessment results and review student needs. The example in Table 3.1 summarizes screening results for a kindergarten class. Results indicated that three students did not meet the benchmarks, with two students showing some risk and one student showing high risk for reading difficulty. It also appears that these students had difficulty with both important areas in reading: phonemic awareness (phonemic segmentation) and phonics (nonsense word fluency). If other assessment data confirm that these students are experiencing difficulty in reading, a systematic supplemental reading intervention should be applied. Ideally, supplemental intervention should include a small group of three to six students (Gersten et al., 2007; Gersten et al., 2009; Kurns & Tilly, 2008).

Step 2:   Choose a supplemental reading intervention that addresses up to three important areas of reading (e.g., phonemic awareness, phonics, comprehension, fluency, vocabulary) that most closely matches student needs. By selecting and preparing to implement several supplemental reading interventions prior to the beginning of the year as indicated in Step 2, the teacher will be well prepared to choose and implement the most appropriate program. It is important to note that, for English language learners, explicit vocabulary instruction is important to overall reading success (Gersten et al., 2007). The supplementary intervention should be implemented using standard protocol. Standard protocol means that the teacher will implement the supplementary intervention or program for the entire small group without determining individual needs through further assessment. If the program or intervention is research based, addresses up to three important areas of reading, and is implemented systematically with integrity, research suggests that this action alone is likely to improve the reading skills on the small group of students at Tier 2 (Gersten et al., 2009). Providing intensive and systematic intervention in the important areas of reading to small groups is reported most often in the literature (Kurns & Tilly, 2008), supported by research, and likely to produce positive results for all students, including English language learners (Gersten et al., 2007, 2009).

Step 3:   Schedule small-group intervention at least three times per week for 20 to 40 minutes each session (Gersten et al., 2009; Kurns & Tilly, 2008) in addition to the core curriculum. If English language learners need intervention, it is appropriate to include them in these heterogeneous groups (Gersten et al., 2007). In other words, it is better to place English language learners with native English speakers. In addition, for English language learners, research suggests that providing instructional activities for at least 90 minutes per week where peers work together on academic tasks is a successful practice (Gersten et al., 2007). If the suggestions in Chapter 1 were followed, a daily schedule for assessment activities is already in place. For example, a second-grade teacher scheduled assessment time for the last 35 minutes of the day. During this scheduled time, while individual students were assessed, other students were engaged in meaningful independent activities. This scheduled assessment time could also be used for supplemental intervention on days when assessments are not scheduled. On days when assessments are scheduled, it would be important to schedule another time for the small-group intervention. It is essential that the additional 20 to 40 minutes of supplemental intervention time (in addition to the core curriculum) be scheduled on a regular basis, with advance planning and organization. Advance planning also includes meaningful activities for other students. Just like the scheduled assessment time, students should be taught the routine so that the activity becomes automatic.

Step 4:   Determine where intervention will occur and who will deliver the intervention. Ideally, intervention will occur in the same location (e.g., at a small table) at routine times for each session. Although the classroom teacher will likely deliver supplementary intervention, it is possible to train parent volunteers or a paraprofessional to deliver a supplementary program or intervention.

Step 5:   Implement intervention systematically for the small group. Each lesson should be explicit (i.e., unambiguous and precise), include a high level of teacher–student interaction, include multiple opportunities for practice, and provide for clear feedback from the teacher (Gersten et al., 2007, 2009).

Step 6:   Integrity should be monitored regularly. Integrity means that the intervention is delivered in the manner expected. Integrity can be monitored by using self-reporting logs, observation by other professionals, and/or use of rating scales. Integrity includes asking the following question: Am I implementing the program according to the program guidelines? One way to check for integrity, for example, would be to construct a simple checklist of the important pieces of instruction using a particular program and then self-assess integrity after delivering a lesson or ask another professional to observe delivery of the intervention.

Step 7:   Student progress will be monitored every other week (as addressed in Chapter 4). After at least 6 to 8 weeks, the teacher will use student progress data (discussed in Chapter 4) to determine if a student should: (a) return to the core curriculum without supplemental intervention (Tier 1), (b) continue the supplemental intervention (Tier 2), (c) increase the minutes of intervention (intensify Tier 2), (d) try a different supplemental intervention (Tier 2), or (e) move the student to Tier 3 for individualized, intensive intervention.

Tier 3

If a student is not responding (i.e., meeting benchmarks or making adequate progress) after receiving the core instruction and research-based supplementary intervention after a reasonable time (6 to 8 weeks), the student might need more intensive instruction (Tier 3). Students who require Tier 3, or more intensive intervention, will continue to receive the core reading curriculum (75 to 90 minutes per day) plus supplemental intervention (three times per week, 20 to 40 minutes per session). It is likely that when a student is in need of intensive reading intervention (Tier 3), other professionals will become involved. For these students, the following steps may be followed:

Step 1:   Contact the building-based assistance team, if one is available, to request assistance in developing an intervention plan. Work through the building team to accomplish Steps 2–4.

Step 2:   Monitor the progress of each student at Tier 3 on a weekly basis. Progress monitoring involves regularly administering a brief assessment using prepared standard probes, like DIBELS (University of Oregon), AIMSweb, or teacher-constructed probes from the curriculum, like CBM (Scott & Weishaar, 2003), or another progress-monitoring assessment. This progress-monitoring procedure will be addressed in Chapter 4.

Step 3:   Continue to provide daily instruction in the core reading curriculum. This might involve providing differentiated instruction to meet student needs.

Step 4:   Continue to provide supplementary intervention at the Tier 2 level. This procedure was described above for Tier 2 in Steps 4–10.

Step 5:   Individualize and intensify intervention for each student at Tier 3. This intensified intervention should have the following characteristics:
- Intervention should occur for individuals or groups of two to four students who have similar needs (the teacher may need to assess students in more depth to clarify specific needs).
- Students should have individualized goals.
- An additional 90 minutes of intervention in reading should be provided on a daily basis (Kurns & Tilly, 2008).
- The intensive intervention should be matched with student needs.

The intensive intervention provided might include special education. In referring a student from Tier 3 to special education, utilize progress-monitoring data to show that the student is not responding to research-based intervention (to be discussed in Chapter 4). Special education involves high-intensity, individualized intervention, in addition to the core curriculum.

PRIORITIZING STUDENT NEEDS BASED ON AVAILABLE RESOURCES

It is important to focus on changes that can be realistically implemented to meet the needs of students given available resources and priorities. To summarize student needs and assist in making decisions, the Table 3.4 charts may be useful. Please note that all actions are high priority because students are directly affected.

TABLE 3.4   Prioritizing Student Needs

Question: Do at least 80% of students meet the reading benchmarks?	
Yes	**No**
Action: Continue to provide the core reading instruction to all students. Continue regular screening for all students three times a year.	**Action:** Review core curriculum, focusing on factors aligned with teaching and learning (discussed at the beginning of this chapter, under Tier 1).
Resources: Additional resources not required	**Resources:** High need (e.g., time, effort, money)
Priority: High	**Priority:** High
Students Affected: All students (80%–100%)	**Students Affected:** All students not meeting benchmarks

Question: Do some students need small-group (Tier 2) intervention?	
Yes	**No**
Action: Apply research-based intervention using standard treatment protocol on a consistent basis. Continue tri-annual screening for all students; Implement progress monitoring at least every other week	**Action:** Continue to provide the core reading instruction to all students; Continue tri-annual screening for all students
Resources: Medium to high need (e.g., time to investigate research-based approaches, time and effort to learn how to implement with integrity—i.e., as intended—possible money to purchase materials)	**Resources:** Additional resources not required
Priority: High	**Priority:** High
Students Affected: Some students (10%–15%)	**Students Affected:** All students

Question: Do some students need individual or very-small-group (Tier 3) intervention?	
Yes	**No**
Action: Implement core instruction and Tier 2 intervention. Consult with building-based team, if available. Consider more intensive intervention from outside sources (e.g., special education). Monitor progress more frequently (weekly).	**Action:** Continue to provide the core reading instruction to all students. Continue tri-annual screening for all students. Continue to implement supplemental research-based intervention for students at Tier 2.
Resources: High need (especially if outside sources are involved)	**Resources:** Medium to high need (to continue implementation of supplementary research-based intervention); low need (to continue implementation of core) curriculum)
Priority: High	**Priority:** High
Students Affected: A few students (1%–5%)	**Students Affected:** All students

Setting Performance Goals

After determining possible actions, resources needed, and priority, it is important to write goals for the desired change. For example, if 85% of students reach the reading benchmarks, the teacher will not develop goals around the core reading curriculum. This doesn't mean that the teacher won't continue to improve instruction and curriculum, only that screening assessment data did not indicate concerns with the response of most students to the core curriculum. However, if several students (i.e., the additional 15% of students) function at Tier 2 (at risk), goals would include the following:

- Plan and prepare lessons using one research-based intervention that focuses on two to four important areas of reading at the appropriate grade level.
- Schedule 20- to 40-minute sessions 3 days per week for implementation of the research-based supplementary program of intervention.
- Monitor progress of these students every other week (Chapter 4) using a progress-monitoring assessment.
- Review and evaluate the effects of intervention over a 6- to 8-week period.
- Restructure groups and increase intensity of interventions based on progress.

In setting and carrying out goals, it is essential to be prepared to systematically implement research-based interventions, plan a weekly schedule for interventions, and monitor the effects of the interventions by charting student performance over time (Chapter 4).

PRACTICAL APPLICATION

CASE 3.1

I Love Teaching Second Grade

I always wanted to be a teacher! After a very busy and successful for 4 years at the local university, I graduated and was offered a position teaching second grade at Rock Elementary School. I remember how thrilled I was when I was offered a teaching position! I taught 4 successful years and was awarded tenure at the end of last year.

In my kindergarten-through-fifth-grade building, there are a variety of teaching styles and curriculums in the area of reading. There is one section of about 25 students at each grade level. As teachers, we agree that we know what is developmentally best practice and appropriate curriculum in reading at each grade level. For example, the kindergarten teacher focuses on immersion in literacy, including phonemic awareness, alphabet knowledge, word knowledge, and listening skills. She is an experienced teacher who taught kindergarten for 20 years and uses her own materials. The first-grade teacher has a strong background in special education and uses a phonics-oriented program, as well as considerable practice with fluency. She adopted a standard basal curriculum. As the second-grade teacher, I feel that students need more work with phonics and comprehension skills. I use a combination of my own phonics worksheets, parts of a different basal reading series, and silent reading using a computer-based program. In third grade, the teacher feels that students should read literature, so the program is solely focused on reading novels silently and understanding vocabulary. The novels are sometimes at higher reading levels than those in third grade, but the teacher feels that all students benefit from this approach, even those who struggle with reading. All of our teachers feel that they successfully teach children in reading, even though we offer very different approaches to curriculum and instruction.

My position this year is somewhat difficult. Our school district is in the process of adopting a new practice, Response to Intervention. Although I believe in the philosophy, especially the belief that all children can learn, I feel that this process is an intrusion into my classroom. I am now told that I must screen all of my students three times a year in reading, track students' progress, use research-based practice, and place students into tiers for instruction. I am already very busy teaching my second-grade students, and I am just not sure how I can handle additional responsibilities. I wonder if this is just another way to decrease the number of students referred for special education.

During the summer, the district offered training in how to carry out assessments for screening and progress monitoring for children in reading. The district opted to use Dynamic Indicators of Basic Early Literacy Skills (DIBELS). Although I was reluctant to participate, I did attend the workshops and learned how to administer the screening assessments and summarize student progress.

It is now the end of September, and I just administered the first screening to my students. It was difficult scheduling these assessments for my students with no additional help, but I completed the screening and summary of my students' scores. As I review my students' scores, the question is, "Now what should I do?" The scores simply don't make sense!

TABLE A: CASE 3.1   Screening Second Grade

Assessment: Fall _X_ Winter_____ Spring_____

Student	Oral Reading Fluency Score*		
	Low Risk	Some Risk	High Risk
John			5
Tim			21
Mary			10
Paul			24
Rahda			18
Pamela			14
Jian			25
Dominique			11
Chavon			9
Valerie			14
Elena			13
Denita			15
Nick			10
Cody			21
Jake			14
Brian			20
Lindsey			13
Kendyl			20
Kelvin			17
Kristin			20
Sandra		40	
Kulaya		31	
Allison	51		
Sheena	48		

I really think there is a problem with this test! Most of my students did not meet the benchmark and are at risk for experiencing difficulty in reading! Only two students met the benchmark. As I think about this, most of my students come from high-poverty families. This, along with the inadequacy of the test, must be the problem. I even wonder if retention might be the answer. If the students had the same curriculum over again, maybe this would help.

In talking with my colleagues in kindergarten, first, and third grades, I am not alone. In kindergarten and first grades, most students meet the benchmarks, but in second and third grades, most students do not meet the benchmarks. We believe that the test is faulty and that it does not reflect what we teach. We agreed to discuss with our building principal the possibility of changing the screening assessment next year. I decided that I will continue screening the children this year, but I will just wait to implement any other strategies until next year, with the exception of potential retention for some students and referral to special education for others.

Questions

1. Interpret the pattern of screening scores for the second-grade class.
2. Do you think this teacher's interpretation is appropriate? Why or why not?
3. Why do you think this pattern occurred? What data support your hypothesis?
4. Describe the problem and one goal to address the problem.
5. List three actions that you would take to further investigate (and possibly substantiate) the problem.

CASE 3.2

What if . . . Parent Recollections of Early Reading

Although James is bright, happy, and successful in school, I will always wonder if his early reading teachers could have done more to improve his reading skills. Don't get me wrong: James can read. It's just that I always think back and wonder if he could have done better with appropriate support. Today, James is a 16-year-old boy who has an average grade point (2.8 out of 4.0), takes college-bound classes (geometry, chemistry, etc.), but is not always academically motivated. Average or above-average grades come with little or no effort. Standardized test scores in eighth grade were 40th percentile in reading and 89th percentile in math. James plans to go to the local university. But I will always wonder. . . .

When James began kindergarten, he loved school and made many friends. It seemed that all of the other children loved him. I remember meeting with James's teacher, Mrs. Cass, at the fall parent conference. She said that he was progressing in an average manner but that he didn't completely understand phonics. She said not to worry about his reading progress. I remember that the curriculum in kindergarten was not centered on one basal reading series but focused on language development, vocabulary, phonemic awareness, early phonics, and simple sight word reading. The teacher was experienced and developed her own curriculum.

In first grade, Mrs. Ryan called me one day and said that during a reading test, James broke down in tears. This was heartbreaking to me because crying about anything was unlike James. He must have felt so frustrated and overwhelmed! The teacher held him on her lap and told him everything was okay, and then she helped him complete the test, item by item. This frustration passed and James seemed to progress in an average manner, even though the teacher again indicated that he had difficulty with phonics. I recall that the curriculum was a blend of teacher-constructed activities focusing on phonics, structured writing activities connected to reading, and a new basal reading series.

In second grade, James had a terrific teacher, who methodically taught word recognition and phonics skills. James still struggled with phonics, but he was able to read on grade level, relying on his strong sight word and vocabulary skills. The teacher, Mrs. Stevens, said that some children simply didn't understand phonics, but they learned to read well. She thought that James was in this category. Although Mrs. Stevens used her own teacher-made phonics activities, she also used the second-grade basal reading series.

In third grade, Mrs. Able seemed to treat the children as if they were in middle school. The reading curriculum consisted on various novels, mostly written on a fourth- and fifth-grade level, with round-robin reading. The focus was on comprehension and vocabulary. I remember that James brought a test home from one chapter in a novel the class was reading. On the left side of the page were 25 vocabulary words and on the right side were 25 definitions. The children had to match the word with the definition. After this activity, the class would read the next chapter. At the end of the book, a written comprehension test, usually with multiple choice items, was given. I vividly remember the teacher calling me one Sunday afternoon stating, "He just isn't doing well in reading. I'm not sure why or what to do." I felt sick when she talked to me.

Now, here we are, many years later. James is successful and independent. Next year, he will prepare to take college entrance exams, and I think he will do well on the tests. I sometimes look back and think, *What would have made a difference his early school years?*

I think James experienced difficulty with phonics from the beginning. I don't think he had a disability, but he probably needed extra intervention in phonics. He was able to compensate by his high ability and his easygoing manner. I think the teachers did not work well together and developed "silos" of curriculum for each grade level. Each teacher taught a curriculum that she thought was best for the children, not necessarily one that was research based and consistent from grade to grade. The kindergarten teacher was excellent and probably did a terrific job, even though she developed most of the curriculum. The first- and second-grade teachers loosely followed two different basal series, but they also used what they thought would help the children by creating activities. The third-grade teacher decided to teach high-level novels, which was a huge leap from the previous grades. There wasn't much coordination of the curriculums, nor was it apparent that any of the curriculums used were evidence based.

Each of these teachers contacted me about James's struggle with phonics, and not one of them offered data to support this conclusion. In addition, none of them told me what she was going to do to correct the difficulty achieving in phonics. I presume that each teacher did something, but this was not articulated. It really would have helped for each teacher to immediately begin providing supplemental intervention for James in phonics early, systematically, and frequently, while tracking his progress. My assessment of how well James achieved in reading was based on anecdotal information from the teachers and his grades.

Although James is progressing well today, I do sometimes wonder how well he would have progressed if the school system would have used the basic principles of Response to Intervention. He still struggles with spelling and writing and doesn't like to read books for pleasure. In my opinion, Response to Intervention is essential to the success of all children.

My personal experience shows why all teachers should be using research-based core reading programs for all students. They should also be assessing students' progress regularly and providing systematic, evidence-based, supplementary intervention for any student who does not meet important reading benchmarks. This practice should be automatic, with no exceptions.

Questions

1. Describe the opportunities for these teachers to incorporate data-based decision making. What should have happened, and when should it have happened?
2. What did the parent mean by "silos" of curriculum? Discuss any experience you have experienced with "silos" of curriculum.
3. What first steps could you take in your classroom to incorporate the core principles of RtI?
4. Why do you think incorporating the core principles of RtI would be helpful in this situation?

How to Implement Reading Assessment for Progress Monitoring in the Elementary Classroom

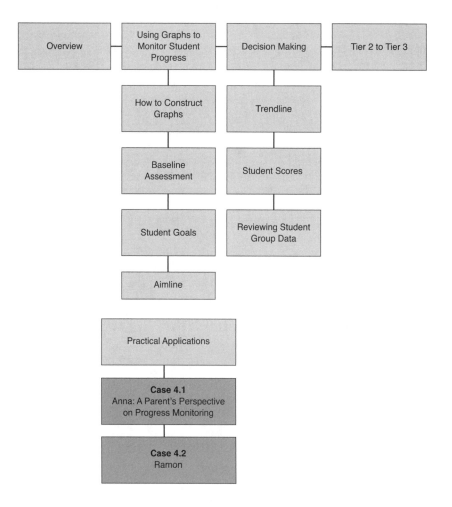

OVERVIEW

Chapter 1 presented an overview of RtI, and Chapter 2 guided the teacher in selecting, organizing, and learning to administer an assessment tool to regularly screen (and monitor the progress of) students in the important areas of reading. Chapter 3 discussed how to review screening results in a meaningful way, make decisions to define problems, and address student needs at Tiers 1, 2, or 3. This chapter addresses the next steps, including how to continually monitor student progress and how to use the resulting data to make decisions at Tiers 1, 2, and 3. To illustrate how progress monitoring fits within the assessment scheme, consider the case scenario of John, a third-grade student.

During the summer, Mr. Tomlinson, John's teacher, prepared assessment materials, learned how to administer the DIBELS oral reading fluency assessment, and selected several evidence-based interventions addressing important areas of reading. At the beginning of the year, Mr. Tomlinson talked with his students and their parents about the rationale for administering screening assessments to all students. About 45 minutes at the beginning of each day was devoted to assessment and/or intervention activities. After the fall screening, John was one of three students who did not meet the oral reading benchmarks for fifth grade. These students' progress was monitored (using DIBELS) for 6 weeks after the screening to confirm the assessment results from the original screening. Based on this confirmation, it was apparent that the three students were not progressing as expected. John and the other two students were placed in a small supplemental learning group (i.e., Tier 2) that focused on the development of vocabulary, fluency, and phonics. This research-supported intervention was implemented in addition to daily instruction in the core reading program. For the supplemental intervention, Mr. Tomlinson worked with the small group 3 days a week for 20 minutes each session. He carefully built skills gradually, working with students explicitly and offering multiple opportunities for teacher–student interaction. While the small group worked, other students independently completed reading center assignments. Every other week, students in this small group were assessed by reading aloud for 1 minute to Mr. Tomlinson using the DIBELS progress-monitoring probes. Afterward, he graphed each student's progress. At the end of 6 weeks, John's progress monitoring assessment results were reviewed, and it was apparent that he had made progress as a result of the intervention by meeting the grade-level established benchmarks. Therefore, John discontinued the supplemental intervention and continued with core reading instruction. John continued to participate in the schoolwide screening assessments three times per year.

The National Center of Response to Intervention defines *progress monitoring* as

repeated measurement of academic performance to inform instruction of individual students in general and special education in grades K–8. It is conducted at least monthly to a) estimate rates of improvement, b) identify students who are not demonstrating adequate progress and/or c) compare the efficacy of different forms of instruction to design more effective, individualized instruction (National Center of Response to Intervention, June 5, 2009, p. 2).

TABLE 4.1 Progress Monitoring

Tier	Purpose	Whose Progress Is Monitored?	Frequency of Progress Monitoring Assessment	How Long Progress Is Monitored Before Decisions About Interventions and Tiers Are Made*
Tier 1	To confirm the existence of reading difficulty—i.e., to validate screening results	*Only* students who do not reach established reading benchmarks based on screening (typically no more than 15% of students)	Every other week	At least 6–8 weeks
Tier 2	To track student progress and effectiveness of supplemental intervention	Students who receive supplemental intervention (typically no more than 15% of students)	Every other week	At least 6–8 weeks
Tier 3	To track student progress and effectiveness of intensive, individualized intervention	Student who receive intensive, individual intervention (typically no more than 5% of students)	Every week	At least 6–8 weeks

*There is no general consensus for duration of progress monitoring before making decisions. Gerston et al. (2009) suggested at least 6 weeks, Fuchs and Fuchs (2007) suggested 6–10 weeks, and Deno, Lembke, and Reschly Anderson (n.d.) recommended 6 weeks. Stecker and Lambke (2005) suggested 4 weeks (and 8 data points) or 3 weeks (and 6 data points).

Progress monitoring may be used to confirm the screening results (as an additional assessment) for students in Tier 1 and/or to track progress for students in Tiers 2 and 3. Although the professional literature suggests that the level of evidence to support monitoring the progress of students at Tier 2 is minimal (Gerston et al., 2009), it is also believed that practitioners need to be aware of student progress to understand the impact of instruction on student learning. To effectively utilize progress monitoring, the following are described in this chapter as related to Tiers 1, 2, and 3:

- How to construct student progress graphs
- How to set individual goals for students
- How to draw and use baseline assessment, aimline (the goal line, or the line between the student's initial score and the student's goal), and trendline
- How to make decisions about instruction based on progress monitoring

Table 4.1 shows when progress monitoring is typically used at Tiers 1, 2, and 3.

USING GRAPHS TO MONITOR STUDENT PROGRESS

How to Construct Graphs

To carry out progress monitoring, a graph should be constructed for each student monitored. The same graph template should be used for each student whose progress is monitored. Regardless of the tool used, a graph's horizontal axis lists the dates that students were assessed. The vertical

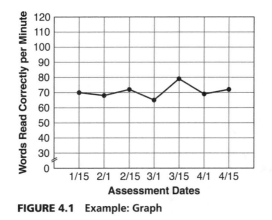

FIGURE 4.1 Example: Graph

axis shows the possible scores on the assessment. Each time a student is assessed, the score for that date is plotted and the dots are connected as each student is assessed over time. For example, when using curriculum-based measurement (CBM) in reading for a fourth-grade student at Tier 2, the sample would look like Figure 4.1.

Teachers can construct graphs by using electronic resources or manually using graph paper. One of the best electronic resources for constructing and using graphs is the Web-based Intervention Central Curriculum-Based Measurement Warehouse (http://www.interventioncentral. org/index.php/cbm-warehouse#graphing).

At this site, a section titled Graphing Options has several valuable links to Paper Graphing Forms, On-Line Graphing (using ChartDog), and Excel Graphs (to create time-series graphs). Another method, using graph paper, involves constructing the graph by hand.

Baseline Assessment

After the graph template is prepared for an individual student, the teacher should conduct baseline assessment. The baseline assessment is descriptive of the level at which the student is performing before implementing any supplemental or intensive intervention. As stated earlier, it is not appropriate to make a decision based on one assessment. Similarly, it is not appropriate to state that a student functions at a particular level based on only one assessment probe. Therefore, several assessment probes are administered over a period of time (e.g., weekly), and the middle score (median) is assumed to be representative of the student's current functioning. Subsequent assessment data are compared to this baseline assessment to determine and show growth. Baseline assessment is conducted in the following manner. The score examples come from DIBELS assessment probes.

Step 1: Three times over a period of 3 weeks (one time per week), conduct the assessment using different probes.

Step 2: Find the median (middle) score for the three baseline assessments. To determine the median score, order the three scores from low to high and choose the middle score. This is the median score. Plot the median score on the student's graph (Figure 4.2) and label it "baseline."

1. Administer the assessment three times

   Dec. 1   Score = 40 correct words per minute
   Dec. 7   Score = 45 correct words per minute
   Dec. 14   Score = 39 correct words per minute

2. Order scores low to high

   Low score   = 39
   Middle score   = 40
   High score   = 45

3. Middle score (median) = 40 correct words per minute (This score is the baseline score and is plotted on the graph as the starting point.)

FIGURE 4.2   How to Compute the Baseline Score

Student Goals

After determining the level at which the student is functioning, the next step is to determine the student's goal so that progress can be measured toward the goal. There are at least two ways to determine goals: The first is the grade-appropriate target of correct responses. This grade-appropriate target is based on research specific to a particular assessment and typically reported in the assessment instruction manual. For example, if using DIBELS, the grade-level target is prominent on the DIBELS graph and designated in a gray shaded area. For a second-grade student, then, the goal would be to read at least 90 words correctly per minute by the end of a school year. If developing an individualized education program goal for special education (Tier 3), the goal would read, "By May 31, given a reading passage from the second-grade DI-BELS oral reading passages, the student will correctly read at least 90 words." This goal could also be appropriate for a student in Tier 2.

The second way to determine a student goal would be to project the typical rate of growth for a student based on grade level. Deno, Lembke, and Reschly Anderson (n.d.) suggested these reasonable weekly improvement rates for oral reading fluency.

- Grades 1–2: 1.5 words per week
- Grades 3–6: 1.0 word per week

Stecker and Lembke (2005) suggested the following weekly realistic increases for oral reading fluency (Table 4.2).

Scott and Weishaar (2003) suggested projecting a weekly increase of one or two words. Any of these are appropriate in projecting student goals.

Using Stecker and Lembke (2005) for a fourth-grade student whose progress will be monitored over a period of 12 weeks and whose baseline oral reading fluency score is 25 (words read correctly per minute), the goal would be 35 (.85 × 12 + 25) = 35.2 This student's goal would be to read correctly 35 words per minute after 12 weeks of intervention. If writing an individualized education program goal for special education (Tier 3), the goal would read, "By December 15, when given a reading passage from the fourth-grade core curriculum, the student will correctly read 35 words per minute." This goal could also be appropriate for Tier 2.

TABLE 4.2   Expected Gains in Reading Fluency

Assigned Grade	Goal for Weekly Increase in Oral Reading Fluency
1	2.0 words per week
2	1.5 words per week
3	1.0 word per week
4	.85 word per week
5	.5 word per week
6	.3 word per week

(*Source:* Adapted from *Advanced Applications of CBM in Reading: Instructional Decision-Making Strategies Manual*, by P. M. Stecker and E. S. Lembke, 2005, Washington, DC: US Office of Special Education Programs)

Aimline

The aimline is the straight line drawn between the baseline median score and the goal. After plotting the baseline median score on the graph, the teacher would draw a straight line, or aimline, between that point and the target or goal. As the student's progress is monitored over time, each assessment probe is plotted on the graph and measured against the aimline. The aimline is illustrated in Figure 4.3.

DECISION MAKING

There are different ways of interpreting student assessment data to make decisions about intervention. Below are two methods that are appropriate for interpreting student data. One is based on interpretation of a trendline, and the other is based on interpretation of consecutive data points.

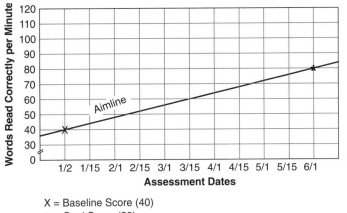

X = Baseline Score (40)
★ = Goal Score (80)

FIGURE 4.3   Example: Aimline

Trendline

The trendline represents a student's actual rate of progress or slope of improvement and is measured against the aimline. Decisions about the intervention's effect on learning can be made using a trendline. To construct a trendline using the Tukey method, Fuchs and Fuchs (2007) suggested these steps.

1. After six to nine points are plotted on the graph, divide the points into three equal sections (or as equal as possible) and draw a vertical line after the first and second groups.
2. Calculate the median point for the first and third sections and mark these on the graph with an X.
3. Draw a straight line between the Xs. This line is the trendline (see Figure 4.4).

To make decisions using a trendline, Stecker and Lemke (2005) suggested the following rules:

1. After a minimum of 4 weeks intervention and a minimum of eight data points (or scores from eight assessments), the trendline and aimline can be compared and decisions made.
   • If the trendline is below the aimline, consider an intervention or instructional change (see Figure 4.5).
   • If the trendline is above the aimline, consider raising the aimline (see Figure 4.6).
2. However, if the following applies, do not use the rule stated above. Instead, follow this rule. After a minimum of 3 weeks of intervention and a minimum of six data points, review the four most recent data points.
   • If these four points are above the aimline, the goal should be increased.
   • If these four points are below the aimline, consider an intervention or instructional change.
   • If these four data points fall above and below the aimline, continue to implement the intervention and monitor progress.

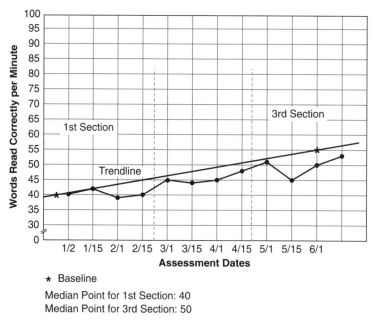

★ Baseline
Median Point for 1st Section: 40
Median Point for 3rd Section: 50

FIGURE 4.4   Example: Trendline

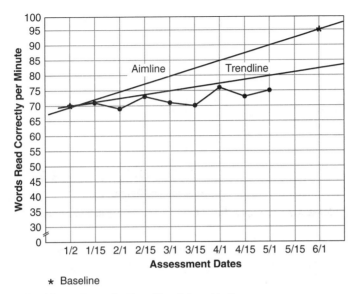

★ Baseline

FIGURE 4.5   **Example: Trendline Below Aimline**

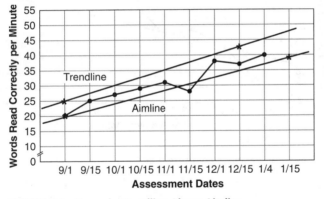

FIGURE 4.6   **Example: Trendline Above Aimline**

Student Scores

The second way of interpreting graphed student assessment data involves reviewing the place-ment of points on the graph. After at least three consecutive probes are administered, the graph can be reviewed and decisions made (Scott & Weishaar, 2003).

- If three consecutive points are below the aimline, consider changes in intervention and/or instruction (see Figure 4.7).
- If three consecutive points are neither consistently above nor below the aimline, no changes should be made (see Figure 4.8).
- If three consecutive points are above the aimline, consider returning the student to the tier above—i.e., Tier 3 return to Tier 2, Tier 2 return to Tier 1 (see Figure 4.9).

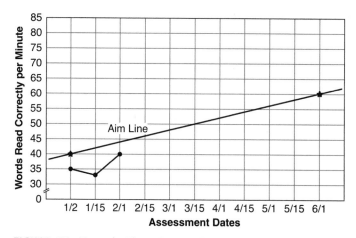

FIGURE 4.7 Example: Three Consecutive Points Below Aimline

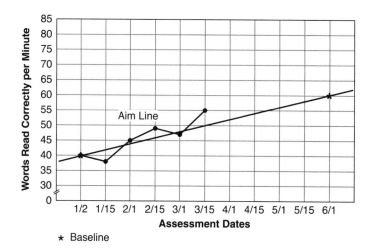

★ Baseline

FIGURE 4.8 Example: Points Neither Above Nor Below Aimline

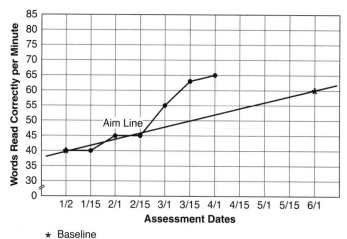

★ Baseline

FIGURE 4.9 Example: Three Consecutive Points Above Aimline

Reviewing Student Group Data

As indicated in Table 4.1, student progress is monitored more frequently for students in Tier 3 than in Tier 2 or for assessment confirmation in Tier 1. For Tiers 2 and 3, after 6 to 8 weeks of intervention and regular progress monitoring, progress should be reviewed and decisions made about the effectiveness of intervention. When reviewing student progress of a small group, the following decision-making model is useful in fine-tuning the intervention.

- If one or two students in the group are not making progress and other students in the group are making progress, it might help to provide additional, more intensive practice and review (5 to 10 minutes) of skills taught for the students not making progress (Gerston et al., 2009).
- If the entire group is not making progress, it would be appropriate to review the intervention. Is the pace too fast? Are the important areas of reading addressed by the intervention (Gerston et al., 2009)?
- If the entire group is making progress, the intervention should be continued. The intervention (and, as appropriate, the additional intensive practice for students who are not making progress) will continue for another 6 to 8 weeks. After this 6- to 8-week period, student progress should be reviewed again.
- If the same student still is not making progress during the 6 to 8 weeks, despite the additional intensive practice and review, it may be appropriate to consider implementing more intensive intervention. If the student is not in Tier 3, it may be appropriate to consider Tier 3 (possibly including a referral for special education). If the student is already in Tier 3, it may be appropriate to seek assistance from the student's individualized education plan (IEP) or building-based team.
- If a student continues to make progress, the intervention should be continued.
- If a student meets the target, the intervention (and frequent progress monitoring) should be discontinued. The student should also be considered for movement to a higher tier.

TIER 2 TO TIER 3

If a student in Tier 2 is not making adequate progress despite adjustments in the intervention, it may be appropriate to refer the student for more intensive, individualized intervention at Tier 3. Tier 3 intervention typically involves special education, although this is not always the case. Tier 3 intervention might involve a building-based team of professionals who review assessment data and determine the most appropriate intensive and individualized intervention. It is very important that the transition between Tier 2 and Tier 3 (e.g., the special education evaluation) be seamless, and efficient. In Tier 2, the student received small-group intervention focused on several important areas in reading instruction. The student's progress was monitored, and data indicated that the student was still not progressing as expected, despite the research-based intervention. In Tier 3, decisions are made by a team of professionals as to the intensity of the individualized intervention (e.g., special education), usually provided, in part, by a specialist. Tier 3 intervention may also include the continuation of Tier 2 intervention and core reading instruction.

For special education referral, the following steps are typical even though school districts have some flexibility in the specific forms and procedures used to determine if a student has a disability and needs Tier 3 intervention.

1. *Complete a formal written referral for special education.*   Usually, the classroom teacher initiates this formal referral and the student has been involved in Tier 2 intervention. This

information should be reflected in the referral. Graphs showing student progress should be attached to the referral. Formal referrals typically include indentifying information, language spoken in the home and by the child, reason for referral, and current instructional levels. After a referral for special education is completed, an IEP team meeting convenes to determine if the referral should result in an evaluation for special education. The IEP team includes the following participants: student's parent or guardian, regular education teacher, special education teacher, special education supervisor and/or administrator, professional who can interpret the instructional implications of assessment data, other persons as appropriate, and the student, if appropriate. Figure 4.10 shows an example of a completed referral.

2. *If the IEP team determines that the referral is appropriate, the team first requests written consent for the evaluation from the parent or guardian. Then the team determines if additional evaluation data are needed to determine if the student has a disability and is eligible for special education.* Teams typically review existing evaluation data, including information from the parent, classroom assessments, and state or local assessments. If additional data are needed, the team determines the type of information that is needed and who is responsible for gathering the information. Assessment data gathered must be nondiscriminatory, focus on educational needs, be comprehensive and multidisciplinary, be valid and reliable, and protect

---

Student Name: Chancellor Brown **Birth Date:** 5/16/99 **Chronological Age:** 11 **Sex:** M **Grade:** 5 **Parent/Guardian:** Wilma Brown **School:** Wilson Elementary **Address:** 105 Curb Court **Telephone:** 791-2222 **Language Spoken in the Home:** English **Language Spoken by the Student:** English **Principal:** Jane Purdue **Person Requesting Evaluation:** John Jacobson, fifth-grade teacher

Reason for Referral: Chancellor has difficulty in reading. He struggles in sounding out words at the fifth-grade level. His oral reading is slow and laborious.

Current Grades:
Reading: D– Mathematics: C+ Social Studies: C– Language Arts: C– Science: C PE: A
His transcript is attached.

Current Assessment Data:
Attachment: Graph showing oral reading fluency progress between September 10 until December 15. Target was 124 words orally read (fifth-grade level) per minute. The baseline for Chancellor was 50 words per minute.

All assessment points fell below the aimline.

Other assessment data: State achievement test (October) showed "below standards" results in reading and "met standards" in mathematics.

Interventions:
Chancellor was screened using the DIBELS Oral Reading Fluency assessment in September. Based on this score and his other assessment test scores (see above), he was placed in Tier 2 intervention in reading. He was a member of a small group of three students who worked in the Academy of Reading program (Autoskill). The group worked in 20 minute sessions, three times per week, for 12 weeks. Progress was monitored every other week. His progress monitoring graph is attached. In addition, Chancellor continued to participate in the core reading program 1 hour per day. Although the program addressed the five important areas of reading (phonemic awareness, phonics, fluency, vocabulary, and comprehension), Chancellor experienced significant difficulty with phonics.

FIGURE 4.10   Example: Completed Special Education Referral

student rights. Using the referral example in Figure 4.10, it is possible that the team decided to gather more information from the parent for a health and social history. Because the student participated in Tier 2 intervention and regular progress monitoring, additional assessment data might not be necessary.

3. *The IEP team determines eligibility for special education.*   In a meeting, the team considers all assessment data and determines whether the student has a disability. In the eligibility determination, Tier 2 intervention and progress-monitoring data are essential in determining if the student has a disability. If the student did not respond to research-based intervention, it is possible that the student could become eligible for learning disability services.

4. *If the student has a disability, the student's educational needs are then specified in a written IEP.*   The team determines the services that are needed to address the student's individual needs. In the scenario presented in Figure 4.10, Chancellor might need individual, intensive intervention from the special education teacher daily in 30-minute sessions focusing specifically on phonics. It might also be determined that Chancellor would benefit from continuing in the core reading program and the supplemental intervention program. The special education teacher, in Chancellor's case, would continue progress monitoring on a weekly basis. Individual goals would be determined in reading. Chancellor's program would be reviewed at least on an annual basis. An individual goal for Chancellor might be, "In 12 weeks, Chancellor will read 75 words correctly per minute using fifth-grade core reading materials."

As previously stated, special education services and referral might not be the only option for Tier 3 intervention. It is possible that other services could be provided outside of special education, like the services of a reading specialist. The important factor would be that a team of professionals worked together collaboratively to intensify, specialize, and individualize intervention, along with monitoring progress more frequently.

This chapter addressed progress monitoring and data-based decision making at Tiers 1, 2, and 3. Chapter 5 discusses important concepts and implications of schoolwide RtI change as it relates to an individual teacher implementing RtI in the classroom.

PRACTICAL APPLICATION

CASE 4.1

Anna: A Parent's Perspective on Progress Monitoring

Background

My husband and I adopted our only child, Anna, when she was 10 months old from China. I will never forget how happy we were when we received photos of her from the adoption agency! She was abandoned as an infant on the doorstep of the orphanage with a short note explaining that her parents could not afford another child. We enthusiastically prepared Anna's room and left for China to bring her home. It was quite a shock when we arrived to see Anna for the first time because she physically looked like a 6-month-old baby and wasn't able to stand up or speak. Apparently, she was well cared for in the orphanage, although we understood that she spent considerable time in her crib. One particular caretaker bonded with Anna, and she was with her daily for the first 10 months of her life. The day after our arrival, my husband and I were ushered to a meeting room with other new parents. Caretakers from the orphanage arrived with the children. Anna's caretaker handed Anna to us, kissed Anna, and then walked out of the room. Anna screamed and literally continued to do so for weeks! It was obvious that Anna was stricken with fear, having been left with strangers by the person with whom she was closely bonded. My husband and I were terrified about our decision to take Anna in these circumstances, but we decided to continue in our journey. I will never forget that day.

It took many months to build trust with Anna, and I took a leave of absence from my position to stay at home. Finally, after over a year, Anna bonded with me and my husband, but she did not want to be left with anyone else. Therefore, I decided to leave my job and stay home with Anna until she began kindergarten.

Kindergarten

Anna entered kindergarten at age 5, and it was quite an adjustment. Anna experienced difficulty relating to other children and separating from me. She cried daily for several weeks! The teacher, Mrs. Bobbit, was aware of Anna's background, and she worked closely with me to ease Anna's adjustment. By late September, Anna was playing with other children and following the classroom routine.

In October, I met with Mrs. Bobbit to discuss Anna's progress in early reading. She explained that all children in her classroom were taking screening tests in early reading during the year in an effort to determine if any of them were experiencing difficulty so that early intervention could occur. At the parent conference, Mrs. Bobbit showed me Anna's screening results. She explained that Anna took two tests from an assessment called Dynamic Indicators of Basic Early Literacy Skills. Anna's scores on the two tests, initial sound fluency and letter-naming fluency, were below expectations. On the first test, initial sound fluency, a series of four pictures was shown, and Anna had to tell which picture began with a particular initial sound. On the second test, letter-naming fluency, Anna had to read the names of letters from a list of letters. Anna's scores on both tests indicated that she may be at some risk for developing difficulty in reading. Mrs. Bobbit said that she wanted to confirm that Anna was really experiencing difficulty in reading with another assessment, and she indicated that she would monitor Anna's progress for about 6 weeks and then contact me to discuss the results.

In December, just before the holiday break, I again met with Mrs. Bobbit. She showed me Anna's progress-monitoring graph on initial sound fluency. She explained that the other test, letter-naming fluency, was only used for screening.

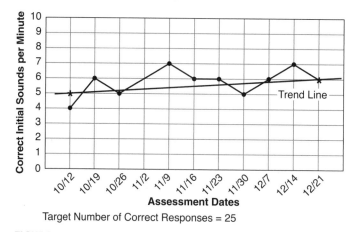

Target Number of Correct Responses = 25

FIGURE A: CASE 4.1 **Anna: A Parent's Perspective on Progress Monitoring**

She explained that Anna took the initial sound fluency test every 2 weeks beginning October 12 and ending December 21. I was reminded that this test was intended to confirm Anna's initial screening results on this test. Each time Anna took this test, her scores were plotted on the graph and the dots were connected. The target number of correct initial sounds per minute for a student in kindergarten was 25. The blue line on the graph showed the overall trend of Anna's progress. Mrs. Bobbit said that Anna's scores over time on this test were below the target of 25 and her overall progress toward the target was slow. These results confirmed that Anna was at risk for having difficulty in reading. Mrs. Bobbit suggested that Anna receive supplemental intervention for the remainder of the school year. Mrs. Bobbit would work with a small group of three children four times a week for 20 minutes each session on early reading skills like initial sound fluency and phonemic awareness. I anticipated meeting with Mrs. Bobbit at the end of May to discuss Anna's progress.

Questions

1. Why was progress monitoring used?
2. At what tier would Anna function at the end of this scenario? How do you know?
3. How could the teacher tell that Anna was not making adequate progress?
4. How will the teacher proceed with progress monitoring when applying supplemental intervention with Anna?

CASE 4.2

Ramon

It was the end of May and I felt somewhat nervous as the individualized education plan meeting began. Participants included George Yu, the school psychologist; Mary Taylor, the special education supervisor; Phil Weis, the school social worker; Bill Workman, school principal; James Wilson, special education teacher; and Mrs. Martinez, Ramon's mother. After introductions, Mary Taylor began the meeting.

MARY TAYLOR: Ramon is a fourth-grade student who has attended King Elementary since kindergarten. He was referred for a full individualized evaluation in April for difficulty with reading. The purpose of our meeting today will be to review assessment information on Ramon and determine if he needs more intensive special education services. As Ramon's fourth-grade teacher, Mrs. Bolden, could you help us understand Ramon's current functioning in your class?

MRS. BOLDEN: Ramon has been in my fourth-grade class all year. He displays much strength. His social skills are exceptional, and he has many friends. On the playground, Ramon is always chosen as a leader in group sports, like soccer and basketball. He encourages other students to keep trying and to help the team. Even if his team loses a game, Ramon is encouraging! Academically, Ramon functions in an average manner in mathematics. He always completes homework, earning As and Bs on most assignments and tests.

However, in reading, Ramon struggles. At the beginning of the year, I reviewed his temporary file and noticed that scores on the state proficiency test in reading were "below standards," which meant that Ramon demonstrated only basic knowledge in reading. His third-grade group achievement test scores in reading, from the Iowa Test of Basic Skills, showed a standard score of 75, which is considered low average in comparison to other children his age. In September, Ramon participated in the reading screening conducted with all students in my class. He was asked to read aloud for 1 minute from fourth-grade reading materials. The expectation for fourth graders was to read at least 95 words per minute, and Ramon was able to read 72 words per minute. This reading score was a concern and was confirmed when compared with reading assessments (state test and Iowa Test of Basic Skills) from third grade. Therefore, my judgment was that intervention was necessary for Ramon in reading. Ramon was then placed in a group of three students who needed intervention in reading within my class. I chose a reading program that research showed to be highly likely to improve reading scores and set aside 20 minutes three times week to implement the program. Before I started implementation, I conducted three separate reading probes with Ramon, where he read aloud for 1 minute. Of the three probes, I took the middle score, 73, as his baseline score, or where he would begin prior to intervention. Then I projected the number of words that I would expect him to gain after 12 weeks of intervention, one additional word per week, or 85 words. Here is Ramon's graph, showing where he began and where he was projected to be after 12 weeks. The straight line, or aimline, shows where I wanted Ramon to be after 12 weeks. Every other week, I monitored his progress so that I could evaluate the effect of the intervention on his progress in reading. As you can see from this graph, Ramon's scores were far below the aimline.

I am concerned about Ramon's reading progress. After 12 weeks of intervention, it is clear to me that he is not responding to the additional intervention. I think he needs more intensive and individualized intervention.

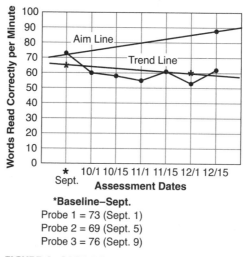

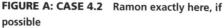

FIGURE A: CASE 4.2   Ramon exactly here, if possible

MARY TAYLOR: Thank you, Mrs. Bolden. When this referral was made, as a team we decided that we needed more information about Ramon's individual reading needs and his health and social history. Mr. Wilson, could you review the additional assessment information in reading?

JAMES WILSON: Yes, I administered the Informal Reading Inventory to Ramon to further define his individual strengths and weaknesses. In oral reading, he displayed the following.

Primer-Level	Word recognition = 100%
	Comprehension = 100%
Level 1	Word recognition = 95%
	Comprehension = 88%
Level 2	Word recognition = 92%
	Comprehension = 73%
Level 3	Word recognition = 90%
	Comprehension = 71%
Level 4	Word recognition = 80%
	Comprehension = 11%

The error pattern suggests that Ramon has difficulty sounding out words phonetically. He will often get the first and last sounds correct but miss the middle sounds. Occasionally, he substituted a word that made sense in the sentence but that was a very different word, like *kid* for *child*. Ramon also was asked to read silently several selections and answer comprehension questions. For these selections, his scores were as follows:

Primer = 100% comprehension
Level 1 = 95% comprehension
Level 2 = 80% comprehension
Level 3 = 70% comprehension
Level 4 = 25% comprehension

These results were consistent with his oral reading. I also read selections to him aloud and he was then asked to answer questions as an assessment of his listening comprehension. Here are the results:

Level 1 = 100% comprehension
Level 2 = 100% comprehension
Level 3 = 95% comprehension
Level 4 = 95% comprehension
Level 5 = 85% comprehension

It appears to me that Ramon is able to understand a reading selection read aloud to him, but his comprehension is hindered by phonetic ability in sounding out words when he reads both silently and orally. Ramon does not appear to be making adequate progress in the classroom with only the supplemental, small-group intervention. I think he could benefit from more intensive reading intervention.

MARY TAYLOR: Thank you, Mr. Wilson. Mr. Weis, you and Mrs. Martinez talked about Ramon's social and health background. Would you share this information?

MR. WEIS: Yes, of course. Mrs. Martinez and I met 2 weeks ago in her home to discuss social and health information. Mrs. Martinez, please feel free to add more information as I summarize our conversation. Ramon was born at home in an uncomplicated birth, and he appears to have met developmental milestones within an average range. Ramon is the youngest of four children. Two of his older sisters are in high school, and his older brother graduated from high school and works for an uncle in a car repair business. Mrs. Martinez emigrated from Mexico when she was 20 and works as a hotel housekeeper. Her husband, Ray, works on a farm. The children are bilingual, speaking both Spanish and English fluently. None of the children had difficulty learning English, although Ramon was part of an intensive English program during kindergarten. After kindergarten, it was determined that he did not need further assistance with English. Ramon and the other children help at home with daily chores. Ramon often helps his mother with dinner, as well as feeding the dog. Ramon's hearing and vision have been screened twice, once in kindergarten and once in fourth grade. He passed both screenings. Mrs. Martinez, can you think of anything I left out?

MRS. MARTINEZ: No.

MR. WEIS: Thank you.

MARY TAYLOR: We need to answer several questions to determine if Ramon needs more intensive and individualized intervention:

1. What is the discrepancy between Ramon's performance in his fourth-grade class and the standard he is expected to meet?
2. What is Ramon's rate of improvement in reading?
3. What are Ramon's educational needs?

Questions

1. How did Mrs. Bolden confirm Ramon's screening test score? Why was this important?
2. How did Mrs. Bolden calculate Ramon's trendline?
3. Do you agree with Mrs. Bolden's conclusion that Ramon was not responding to the intervention? Why or why not?
4. How would you answer each question posed at the end of this case? Support your answers with data from the case. If not able to answer a question, determine what additional data would help you answer the question.
5. Based on the information provided, does Ramon have a learning disability? If so, how do you know?
6. Write one individual education goal for Ramon in the area of reading.
7. What should happen next?

5

Within the Context of Schoolwide Change

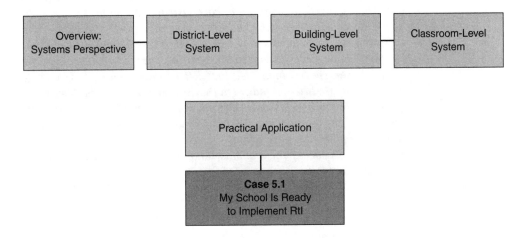

OVERVIEW: SYSTEMS PERSPECTIVE

Mr. Shelton has been implementing RtI in his third-grade classroom in the Whitting School District for the past year. Last year he spoke to his principal, Ms. Denting, about implementing RtI schoolwide in their K–3 building, but she felt it was too expensive given the economic crisis in the district. Mr. Shelton decided to implement RtI in his classroom without schoolwide support and has experienced considerable success over the past year. He used DIBELS to assess all of his students because it was free and easy to use. He determined that of his 30 students, 5 were at risk of learning difficulties and 2 were already experiencing difficulties in reading. To address the needs of the seven students, he implemented a research-based, commercially available reading program in addition to the core curriculum. This program was implemented three times a week for 20 minutes each session. Mr. Shelton monitored the progress of the seven students receiving supplemental intervention on a biweekly basis. By the end of the year, five of the seven students receiving the supplemental intervention program in addition to core instruction had performed well enough to return to core instruction only. The other two students will continue with supplemental intervention. No students were referred for a special education evaluation.

Mr. Shelton took the data to Ms. Denting, the principal, again at the end of his successful year. He recommended that RtI be implemented in Grades K–3 for the following year. Mr. Shelton indicated that the cost was minimal given the successful implementation in his class. Ms. Denting was impressed and indicated that she had been hearing and reading about RtI in the past year and was considering implementation training for the next school year. She had heard that for schoolwide implementation to be successful, she must take a leadership role in its implementation, which is precisely what she intended to do with Mr. Shelton's help.

Although a teacher can successfully implement essential elements of RtI within an individual classroom, implementation on a schoolwide basis has greater impact on more students. To provide a framework for systemwide change, Weishaar, Borsa, and Weishaar (2007) discussed viewing change from a systems perspective. Using this perspective, the concept of circular causality (Becvar & Becvar, 1982) becomes important. Circular causality means that people, events, and systems reciprocally affect one another. To effect change throughout the school district, several primary systems are involved: the classroom system (i.e., children and teacher within one classroom), the school building system (i.e., all administrators, teachers, children, and staff in the building), and the districtwide system (i.e., all administrators, teachers, and staff in the district). Other systems also are important, such as the family system and the administrative system. All systems are interrelated when the reading achievement of children is involved. A change in one system can affect other systems. In the scenario above, Mr. Shelton's successful use of RtI within his classroom effected a change in the building principal's attitude about RtI. It is possible that Mr. Shelton's success with RtI could potentially effect change within other classrooms in his building. The success of RtI on a schoolwide basis involves three stages within the interrelated systems: consensus building, infrastructure building, and implementation (Kurns & Tilly, 2008; Elliott & Morrison, 2008). Building consensus involves discussion, development of a rationale for implementation, and communication of RtI concepts. Building infrastructure involves analysis of current practice, determination of what needs to occur for successful RtI implementation, and filling the gap between current practice and what needs to occur.

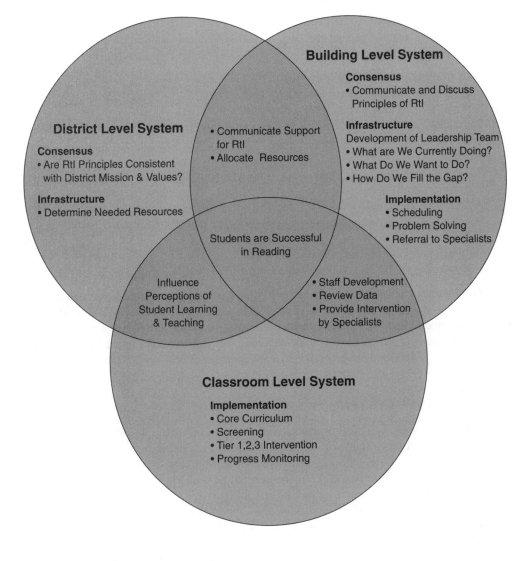

District Level System

Consensus
• Are RtI Principles Consistent
  with District Mission & Values?

Infrastructure
• Determine Needed Resources

Building Level System

Consensus
• Communicate and Discuss
  Principles of RtI

Infrastructure
Development of Leadership Team
• What are We Currently Doing?
• What Do We Want to Do?
• How Do We Fill the Gap?

Implementation
• Scheduling
• Problem Solving
• Referral to Specialists

• Communicate Support
  for RtI
• Allocate Resources

Students are Successful
in Reading

Influence
Perceptions of
Student Learning
& Teaching

• Staff Development
• Review Data
• Provide Intervention
  by Specialists

Classroom Level System

Implementation
• Core Curriculum
• Screening
• Tier 1,2,3 Intervention
• Progress Monitoring

FIGURE 5.1   Systems Perspective and RtI

Implementation involves making sure that appropriate structure and supports are in place for successful RtI implementation. All three systems overlap in the desired outcome that all students are successful in learning to read. Figure 5.1 is a Venn diagram that illustrates systems perspective as related to RtI. Each system, district, building, and classroom is then described.

DISTRICT-LEVEL SYSTEM

The district-level system consists of the board of education, superintendent, and other district-level administrators. Board of education members represent the community and are charged with setting policy for the school district. For RtI, the district-level system is involved primarily in consensus and building infrastructure as well as determining consistent policies. Building consensus includes discussion and general agreement with the important principles of RtI that were discussed in Chapter 1 and are listed again below (National Association of State Directors of Special Education, 2006):

1. Each student can be taught and can learn.
2. Early intervention is necessary.
3. Services are best delivered in several different "tiers."
4. For students to move from one tier to another, employing a problem-solving method is useful.
5. Teachers should use evidence- or research-based instruction and interventions as much as possible.
6. Student progress should be monitored and used to adjust instruction.
7. Data from student progress (and other sources) should be used to make decisions.
8. Assessments are typically used for three different purposes:
   - *Screening* for all students to identify those who are not progressing as expected
   - *Conducting diagnostic* or more *in-depth assessment* to determine what students can and cannot do in academic and behavior areas
   - *Monitoring progress* of students to determine if they are learning at expected rates

An important element for the district-level system to address would be the extent to which RtI principles are consistent with school district vision and mission. Based on the development of consensus around RtI principles, the district-level system would communicate support for RtI and allocate needed resources for RtI implementation. Needed resources might initially involve a districtwide staff-development program and assessment resources.

BUILDING-LEVEL SYSTEM

The building system consists of all personnel within the building, including teachers, specialists, and administrators. An important stage at the building level is developing consensus. During the consensus-building stage, the building-level administrator provides information about RtI and surveys the staff to determine the level of commitment and need for staff development. To move forward with RtI implementation, school personnel must see the value in the initiative and believe that they have the skills or will receive the support to learn the skills to incorporate the initiative into their teaching (Batsche, n.d.). Part of the rationale for RtI implementation might also include teachers' understanding of the relationship between student performance and teacher retention in the Race to the Top Initiative implemented by the Obama administration. With data, teachers are in a position to track student performance in reading.

The next stage, development of the infrastructure, is best led by a building leadership team. The leadership team is critical to the success of RtI implementation within the building. Potential leadership team members, their roles, and their responsibilities are described in Table 5.1.

The purpose of the leadership team is to guide building staff through the system-change process and implementation of data-based decision making on a building-wide basis. The leadership team asks three questions:

1. What is current practice within the building (assessment, intervention, progress monitoring, data-based decision making)?
2. Where do we want to be in terms of implementation of RtI?
3. What is needed to fill the gap between our current building practices and implementation of RtI?

TABLE 5.1   Roles and Responsibilities for Leadership Team Members

Potential Building-Level Person on the Leadership Team	Role on Leadership Team	Primary Responsibility
School psychologist, reading specialist, or special education teacher	Data mentor (should have knowledge of data analysis)	Assist in setting parameters for data collection, analysis, interpretation, and summaries
Classroom teacher or reading specialist	Content specialist (should have knowledge of research-based reading interventions, core instruction, and fidelity)	Assists teachers in using data to improve intervention and improving core reading instruction
Classroom teacher	Facilitator (should use good communication and conflict-resolution skills and have knowledge of collaboration/consultation models)	Supports needs of staff as they move through the transition from the old system to the new system; assures that the leadership team considers input from teachers in the building
Classroom teacher(s)	Staff liaison (could represent multiple grade levels and/or programs)	Provides feedback to and gathers it from those not in the leadership team
Building administrator	Instructional leader (has knowledge of RtI and is committed to RtI)	Has authority to commit district and building resources to support RtI; supports staff in the implementation of RtI
Classroom teacher or administrator	Implementation coach	Liaison to district level system; ensures that leadership team has support and assistance from district-level system
Parent	Parent representative	Communicates with teachers and other parents about RtI

(*Source:* Information from Kurns and Tilly, 2008)

Specific activities of the leadership team include, but are not limited to, the following (Kurns & Tilly, 2008):

General Activities of Coordination and Communication

- Conduct ongoing needs assessments to ensure smooth implementation of RtI.
- Communicate successes, barriers, and challenges to stakeholders.
- Collect, analyze, interprets, and summarize assessment data in such a way that teachers and other stakeholders can understand.
- Coordinate ongoing professional development on RtI.

Core Curriculum

- Review the core curriculum to determine strengths and weaknesses in addressing the state standards.
- Make recommendations for changes in the core curriculum to ensure alignment with state standards.

Assessment

- Select screening tools and assist in coordinating universal screening of all students.
- Determine building-level cut scores at which students will exceed, meet, and not meet expectations of the building.
- Determine the management system that will be used for progress monitoring.

Supplemental and Intensive Intervention

- Select supplemental and intensive research-based materials and interventions.
- Develop the framework for delivering supplemental and intensive instruction within the building (i.e., research-based materials to be used, who will teach what, when supplemental instruction is to be provided, where it is provided, how frequently it is provided, how integrity will be monitored, and the specifics on how the process will be documented).
- Set criteria for when intervention changes will be made based on student performance.
- Serve as a problem-solving team for students who need intensive intervention.
- Assist classroom teachers in referring students for Tier 3 intervention.

CLASSROOM-LEVEL SYSTEM

The classroom-level system is responsible primarily for implementation of the core curriculum, systematic screening of all students (and confirmation assessment for those who do not meet reading benchmarks), tiered interventions, and regular progress monitoring. The details of implementation are the subject of this text. It is important to remember that the classroom system overlaps with the building-level system. For example, staff development coordinated and initiated by the building leadership team benefits the classroom teacher. For students who need more intensive intervention (Tier 3), the building-level leadership team could assist the teacher in determining needed interventions or referral to a specialist. Likewise, the classroom-level system interacts with the district-level system in terms of providing information on classroom-level student learning and teaching.

RtI is an evidence-based practice that requires a paradigm shift in how school districts, school buildings, and teachers view student learning. Many school systems educate students using a dual approach: special education and general education. RtI brings the two systems together to create a unitary system that focuses on *all* school personnel being responsible for the progress of *each* student. Teachers and other education professionals combine resources to track student performance data so that decisions can be made about how to address the needs of all students.

RtI can be implemented in isolation of the schoolwide system, but to ensure maximum benefit for all students, it is better if it is part of integrated district and schoolwide systems. Implementation includes a philosophy of education that focuses on early intervention. It is a paradigm shift away from a dual, segregated system requiring eligibility for special education prior to supplemental and/or intensive intervention to a unitary system that requires intervention and progress monitoring at the first indication of potential risk of academic or behavioral difficulties. RtI moves away from categorizing and labeling students to a system of addressing needs when they occur and, in many cases, preventing the need to categorize students. RtI places the responsibility for learning on the teacher instead of only on the student.

PRACTICAL APPLICATION

CASE 5.1

My School Is Ready to Implement RtI

My school, Jones Elementary School, will begin implementing RtI schoolwide this fall. We have consensus among the teachers in my building to initiate RtI, but I don't think our district has prepared us very well for the rationale behind implementing it. The rationale given last year was, "It's coming" and "We will be doing it." I believe that the teachers and staff in my building have accepted the fact that RtI is happening, even if we don't completely understand why we have to do it.

During the past spring, a leadership team was established in my building. This team consisted of the principal, social worker, reading specialist, and one teacher. They have been meeting weekly during their lunch period. I think the teacher is the data mentor, the reading specialist is the content specialist, the social worker is the facilitator, and the principal is the staff liaison. I'm not sure what they have discussed, and I don't know if the team has received any specific training.

Last year, all elementary teachers attended four districtwide professional development meetings on RtI. At our January teachers' institute, the special education director presented an overview of RtI. He stated that RtI would decrease the number of referrals to special education and allow teachers to work with students who have reading difficulties within the classroom. The district administrators then dictated the research-based assessments we will be using this year. I think they chose AIMSweb to screen all students and monitor progress. Other than an overview, there has not been much training on how to administer the assessments, but teachers in my building will be trained on administration of AIMSweb at a series of teachers' institute days prior to the beginning of the school year.

At the February and March teachers' institutes last year, several teachers presented and discussed district-approved reading interventions for Tier 2, including *Read Naturally* and *Jolly Phonics*. The reading specialist and I shared two programs that we believe are successful for Tier 3 intervention: *Visualizing and Verbalizing* (Lindamood-Bell) and *LiPS* (Lindamood Phoneme Sequencing Program). I think we are prepared to implement interventions.

My principal has been an excellent leader and encouraged teachers in my building to implement RtI. During our April school-improvement day last year, she organized grade-level meetings to review a proposed RtI schedule for this year. We also voted on when we would begin the program this year, in August or January. The entire teaching staff was unanimous on starting on the first day of school in August, hence the full consensus in my building to implement RtI.

During our May professional development day, my principal presented the final RtI schedule. Each grade level will have an hour of time daily where all teachers work on Tier 1 instruction and Tier 2 interventions. Tier 3 interventions will be provided during the same time by the reading specialist. In addition, a 30-minute block at the end of the day is reserved for Tier 3 interventions that will be provided by the reading specialist and the special education teachers. Fridays will be the assessment day, when the reading specialist will check Tier 3 progress weekly and the general education teachers will check Tier 2 progress every other week. The general education teachers will also screen all students three times a year. The teacher on the leadership team has folders and checklists for assessments prepared for every teacher, and I am sure the leadership team has a plan for initiating the assessments, reviewing the data, decision making, and monitoring and evaluating the implementation process as we get everything started.

My principal has excellent communication with our staff, and she recognizes and celebrates the staff throughout the year. I am certain that she will continue to do the same in regards to our RtI implementation.

I believe my school is demonstrating all of the key components necessary to begin successful schoolwide RtI implementation in the fall. Although I'm not completely sure what my specific activities will be as a third-grade teacher, I am confident that someone will tell me before school begins.

Questions

1. Describe and discuss consensus, infrastructure, and implementation of RtI within this district-level system.
2. Describe and discuss consensus, infrastructure, and implementation of RtI within the building-level system.
3. Describe and discuss consensus, infrastructure, and implementation of RtI within the classroom-level system.
4. What are the strengths in this scenario of schoolwide implementation of RtI?
5. What are the challenges in this scenario of schoolwide implementation of RtI?
6. How would you address the challenges?

6

Other Considerations

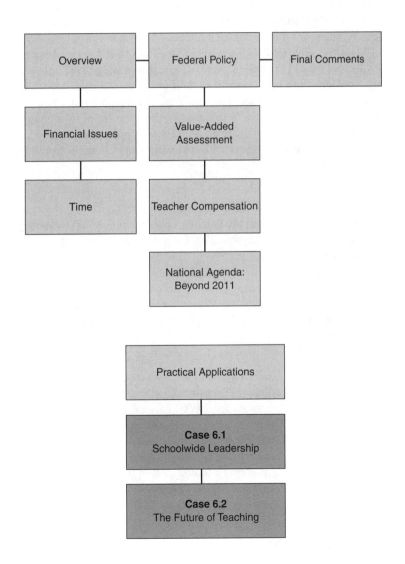

OVERVIEW

When considering the implementation of RtI on a schoolwide basis, issues about the cost of implementation, time involved, the relationship between RtI and other federal education initiatives (e.g., PBIS), current federal funding initiatives (e.g., Race to the Top), and the impact of future federal education legislation (e.g., reauthorizations of the Elementary and Secondary Education Act of 1965 and the Individuals with Disabilities Education Improvement Act of 2004) must be considered. School stakeholders need to discuss these issues prior to implementation on a schoolwide basis.

Financial Issues

The financial cost of implementing RtI is primarily due to purchasing a data-management program such as DIBELS or AIMSWeb. Additional costs are incurred in the purchase of research-based intervention materials that are used for students at Tier 1 and Tier 2. However, this cost is not *only* associated with the implementation of RtI. Even without RtI, schools are required by the No Child Left Behind Act to use research-based curriculum material and to ensure that data are available to document student progress. RtI may reduce the number of referrals for special education, but this potential reduction would not necessarily mean a reduction in special education personnel. Special education personnel time may be reallocated, in part, to assist general education classroom teachers in addressing the needs of all diverse learners in the general education classroom, including students with disabilities and students requiring Tier 2 interventions.

Time

Time is a precious commodity in public schools, and implementation of RtI requires considerable time allocation. Time for professional development, universal screening of students, analysis of student performance data, leadership team meetings, grade-level team meetings, problem-solving team meetings, etc. are important issues associated with the implementation of RtI. However, given the continued and deepening need for accountability, schools will be spending considerable time on efforts to document student progress and the effectiveness of teachers and administrators, with or without RtI. RtI helps to provide this data.

Reallocation of existing resources needed for the implementation of RtI might help to resolve part of the time expense. Consider these reallocations of staff time:

- Utilizing the school psychologist as an assessment specialist for schoolwide achievement may be more efficient than using the school psychologist for evaluating individual students to determine eligibility for special education.
- Utilizing the school social worker to address schoolwide behavior data may prevent individual behavior problems that require extensive individual social-work services.
- Utilizing the reading specialist and special education teacher as leaders in core reading content and instruction or to co-teach in the general education classroom affects all students instead of a few selected students.

In addition, the reallocation of time devoted to professional development on topics that address the needs of teachers at varying stages of RtI implementation may also have a direct positive impact on student performance. In an interview with a prominent early reading expert, Richard Allington (Rebora, 2010), it was suggested that outcomes of high-quality professional development focusing on how to teach reading in the early grades make a difference in the reading achievement of students.

FEDERAL POLICY

The RtI service-delivery model in public school education includes components that are affected by U.S. Department of Education policy and funding incentives and national political efforts to increase public school accountability for student achievement. These components are described in the following summary of the cyclical process of RtI:

- Successful implementation of RtI is based on the premise that school curriculum is aligned with state or national standards.
- Teachers can then assess and evaluate student performance relative to the standards.
- Students who appear to be struggling based on assessments may benefit from research-based supplemental intervention in small groups or individually.
- Teachers utilize the assessment results to monitor student progress over time.
- Assessment results are then utilized to inform teacher decision making about individual instruction for students.

The RtI service-delivery model becomes even more important as President Obama's administration proceeds with efforts to improve the quality of America's schools. Significant proposed changes to the Elementary and Secondary Education Act of 1965 (reauthorized as the No Child Left Behind Act of 2001) focus on major shifts in policy that support RtI and student performance. These proposed shifts in this important law are described in a comparison with the No Child Left Behind Act of 2001 (Table 6.1).

RtI provides schools with the data to document student achievement and rate of learning (growth) over time, which could be used to determine effectiveness of teachers and principals. Assessment data could also be used to document individual student performance and the extent to which achievement gaps are closed. Data could potentially assist schools in convincing school boards to retain teachers, improve student outcomes, and access additional federal funding and flexibility in service delivery under the proposed changes to the Elementary and Secondary Education Act.

Schools that implement RtI systematically analyze their curriculum, align the curriculum with standards, assess students, utilize research-based interventions, and determine if teachers are effective in improving student outcomes. These principles reflect many of the proposed changes in federal policy.

Value-Added Assessment

Because of the shift in federal policy to assessing student growth over time and the potential connection to the teacher, the issue of the value added by the teacher to the student's achievement becomes important. Assessment for accountability usually falls into three categories:

- Norm-referenced assessment, where a student's achievement is compared to other students in his or her grade or age
- Criterion-referenced assessment, where a student's achievement is compared to a predetermined goal or benchmark of achievement
- Value-added assessment, where a student's achievement is compared to his or her expected achievement based on past growth

TABLE 6.1

Issue	Elementary and Secondary Education Act of 2001 (No Child Left Behind)	Proposed Elementary and Secondary Education Act Blueprint (2010 and Beyond)
Focus	No child should be left behind (focus on what should *not* happen)	Every student graduates from high school well prepared for college and a career (focus on what *should* happen)
Accountability	Label and apply serious negative consequences to schools, school districts, and states that fail	Recognize progress and reward schools, school districts, and states that succeed; require change for lowest performing schools and school districts (challenge schools, districts, and states)
Standards	State standards in reading and mathematics	Raise standards for all; promote common standards across states in English language, arts, and mathematics
Assessment	Assessment is an annual snapshot of groups of students; all must meet targets	Assessments will focus on individual student growth and progress over time, as well as annual snapshot; focus on assessment to inform instruction (to respond to academic needs); track growth to a particular teacher
Funding	Distribution formula based on number of students living in poverty	Competitive funding for states, school districts, and schools willing to institute bold reforms (e.g., Race to the Top); flexibility in blending funds
Teachers	Must be highly qualified (bachelor's degree, state certification or licensure, demonstrate subject-matter competency)	Must be highly effective (reward, recognize, encourage excellence); encourage states to implement teacher and principal evaluation and support systems; evaluation systems is intended to inform professional development and improve student learning
Diverse learners	Serious consequences for groups of students who do not meet adequate yearly progress	Support and strengthen programs for all learners and ensure that schools help all students meet college and career-ready standards

Value added refers to an individual student's learning gains from a beginning point (e.g., beginning of school year) to an ending point (e.g., end of school year). Value-added assessment is a process that relates the effectiveness of the teacher to the performance of individual students over time. Value-added assessment focuses less on achievement at the ending point and more on growth over time (from beginning to end of school year). Growth over time is tied to the value a teacher added to the student's learning. Value-added assessment takes into account and attempts to minimize the effects of poverty level, race, and other variables on student growth over time. Typically, value-added assessment computes the projected level of achievement for an individual student at the end of a school year and then compares the student's actual achievement with the projected level of achievement.

Although value-added assessment has been used for many years in special education, since the early 1990s it has been piloted in statewide (e.g., Tennessee, North Carolina) assessment systems (Operation Public Education). Value-added assessment pilot projects now serve as national models for policy shifts in the federal government.

Under the current federal laws, adequate yearly progress (AYP) compares cohorts to cohorts to determine if a school is making AYP goals. In other words, it compares fourth graders in one year to fourth graders from the previous year. Value-added assessment compares an individual student's performance last year to his performance this year and compares his actual performance to his expected performance based on his history of performance. This perspective adds in the value that the teacher added to the student's achievement (Hershberg, 2010).

Teacher Compensation

Data on student performance may be used to determine teacher compensation packages. Teachers whose student data indicate positive outcomes for their students may receive financial compensation for their success. As an example, consider the federally funded grant, Teacher Incentive Fund (TIF), which was created in 2006 to encourage states and school districts to collaborate with nonprofit organizations to implement "performance-based pay systems in high need schools" (Sawchuk, 2010). President Obama's administration will utilize the American Recovery and Reinvestment Act funds in 2010 and 2011 to provide an incentive to states and districts that are willing to implement systems that connect teacher compensation with multiple methods of measuring teacher effectiveness. Both student-achievement data and teacher observations based on performance-based standards will be criteria for grant awards. Grantees will also be required to provide evidence of the following:

- Compensation bonuses change teacher behavior.
- Compensation system change is sustainable after the grant period.
- Multiple methods of improving teacher effectiveness are used.
- Teacher induction and tenure is aligned to teacher effectiveness.
- "Value-added" methodology is used to analyze student test scores over time.
- There is evidence of the recruitment and retention of effective teachers in shortage academic areas.

Access to TIF funds requires support from the teachers' collective bargaining organizations. Both the American Federation of Teachers and the National Education Association indicated that they do not endorse the use of teacher compensation tied to student outcomes but will support local units that choose to bargain the issue (Sawchuk, 2010).

National Agenda: Beyond 2011

Evidence-based practices appear as one central focus of the national education agenda. Data-based decision-making initiatives and teacher reliance on evidence-based practices are becoming the "umbrella" for the process of braiding together similar initiatives such as RtI, positive behavior intervention and supports (PBIS), and individual state initiatives designed to improve academic and behavioral outcomes for students. Assessment of student progress after implementation of evidence-based interventions provides evidence to policymakers and the public that practices used in schools are effective in improving student outcomes. It appears likely that these similar initiatives will be blended together to reduce the redundancy in implementation of initiatives designed to improve outcomes for students. Schools and districts across the country are being inundated with pressure to implement many innovative initiatives as separate entities with their own leadership teams and infrastructure. Scaling up of RtI practices is designed to blend these initiatives into a common system of data-based decision making to allow districts to be more fiscally responsible in documenting federal requirements for student growth analysis. For example, the National Implementation Research Network (NIRN, 2010) provided technical assistance to states in the merging of national, state, and local initiatives to reduce redundancy and promote efficiency of resources. The current focus of NIRN is blending RtI, an initiative that focuses primarily on academics, with PBIS (positive behavioral intervention and supports), an initiative that focuses on behavior. The two initiatives, similar in the use of assessment, progress monitoring, and evidence-based practices, often result in parallel implementation processes and redundancy of resources. NIRN attempts to combine the implementation of these two initiatives into a unitary process. The infrastructure framework incorporates the implementation of all evidence-based practices under an integrated system focusing on student achievement. NIRN has established a framework for this process that has its primary focus of consistency from the state level to the classroom level in the implementation of evidence-based practices that improve the academic and behavior performance of all students and families. The framework at each level is the same and includes selection, training, coaching evaluation, organization supports, and systems integration (NIRN, 2010). At each level, a leadership team is in place to support the leadership team at the next lower level—e.g., state, regional, district, school, grade level (NIRN, 2010). To illustrate the importance of a unitary process, consider the following dilemma.

Waterling School District has a philosophy of ensuring that students in their district meet high academic and behavior expectations. Waterling was a pioneer in the early 1990s in the implementation of PBIS. PBIS is part of a national innovative practice called PBS. The intent of PBIS/PBS is to provide schools with evidence-based practices that will encourage the collection of data on schoolwide discipline, determine building strengths and weaknesses surrounding student behavior, apply research-based interventions to address the weaknesses, and monitor progress over time, all with the goal of increasing appropriate student behaviors without resorting to more restrictive means such as suspension and expulsion. This national innovative practice initiate has formed a foundation for the implementation of RtI.

When RtI was first proposed as a new innovative practice for addressing academic performance, Waterling School District joined the cause to be a state demonstration site. Waterling was awarded the status of demonstration site and began putting together a district-level implementation team. Waterling formed a K–3 team of teachers, administrators, parents, and support staff to begin the consensus-building stage of RtI implementation.

Waterling now has a multiple-district and a building-level teams. They have a district strategic planning team, building-level school-improvement teams, district- and building-level PBIS teams, district- and building-level RtI teams, grade-level teams, problem-solving teams for both academic and behavior, curriculum-development teams, data-analysis teams, administrative teams, and special education referral teams, all of which take up considerable time and involve many of the same individuals. Waterling personnel are worn out trying to keep up with all the innovative practice teams recommended and required by the state education agency. The Waterling special education coordinator, Dr. Basslet, is ready to quit because the redundancy in

responsibilities is overwhelming. Now the state is talking about "evidence-based"
practices.

It is clear from this scenario that school district personnel attempted to apply best practices, but the efforts became fragmented and overwhelming. To fully implement RtI, it is essential that school districts focus on efficiency, best practices, and the well-being of all students.
Viewing RtI as one unitary system of support for all students, both academically and behav-
iorally, helps in the coordination of one system, not multiple systems. In this scenario, it would
be useful to reorganize into one building-system team that includes problem solving, curriculum,
data analysis, special education, and school improvement.

FINAL COMMENTS

There are many advantages of RtI, including the following:

- RtI provides the foundation of an accountability system for documenting and promoting
  individual student achievement and growth in learning over time.
- Combined with behavior-data decision making (i.e., PBIS), RtI allows schools to develop
  an in-depth understanding of student academic and behavior needs and growth over time.
- RtI provides the data for assisting school districts in meeting the intent of upcoming fed-
  eral legislation that helps to document the effectiveness of teachers.
- RtI can be implemented without considerable cost in data-management materials.
- RtI promotes the identification of at-risk students prior to school failure.
- RtI relies on teacher use of research-based interventions.
- RtI provides school districts with data that can be used to compute student growth over time.

At the initial drafting of this book, the economic outlook for public schools appeared grim.
Schools were struggling to meet the federal mandates and provide high-quality education for all
students. The American Recovery and Reinvestment Act (ARRA) stimulus package provided to
public schools in 2008 and 2009 was used to assist districts in funding basic educational programs. By accepting the stimulus money, schools agreed to restructure the delivery of services to
all children. The use of RtI and other evidence-based practices allowed schools to blend federal,
state, and local funds for the benefit of all students. RtI practices provided schools with the data
to determine the most effective means of educating students.

RtI is a process based on the assumption that all children can learn and that all public
school personnel are responsible for the academic and social/emotional success of all students. It
also assumes that a paradigm shift in thinking about public school education is necessary for successful implementation. Under a traditional system, education is a dual responsibility of special
education/remedial teachers and general education teachers. This dual system has separate certification for teachers, separate administrators, separate regulations, separate funding, and separate methodologies of instruction. Under the dual system, students who experience difficulty are
often separated from their peers and educated in separate classrooms by special teachers.

The unitary system, which is one focus of RtI, is one in which teachers are responsible for
the education of each and every student, regardless of the teacher certification held by the
teacher. Teachers are highly effective in teaching all students, and students are not separated
from their peers, unless assessment data demonstrate that the student needs highly intensive,
specialized intervention. All teachers collaborate to address the education of all students.

Students who are not performing as expected receive additional intervention from effective teachers. The unitary system does not have to be more expensive. Schools are more flexible in utilizing personnel to reach all students, whether they are struggling, gifted, or performing as expected. By reallocating how schools utilize existing personnel, all students benefit.

There is a national effort in place to merge the many innovative practices into one system of implementing evidence-based practices in the K–12 schools. Public school innovations come and go, but when implemented appropriately, RtI is a system- or school- or classroom-wide change that can affect positively the learning of all students.

PRACTICAL APPLICATION

CASE 6.1

Schoolwide Leadership

I teach second grade in Marsh Elementary School, and this was my first time as a member of our school leadership team. I wasn't completely sure what to expect. Our school has three sections each of kindergarten, first, second, and third grades. We were meeting for the first time in May to review schoolwide assessment data. Our first task was to discuss the reading achievement of our students. The chairperson of our group explained that we would be reviewing one schoolwide assessment report, the Annual State School Report Card. The first part of the report included descriptive data about our school.

TABLE A: CASE 6.1   Annual State School Report Card—Marsh Elementary

Students—Racial/Ethnic Background (Percent of Total School Population)					
White	Black	Hispanic	Asian or Pacific Islander	Native American	Multiracial or Ethnic
53	25	21	1	0	0

Students—Other Information (Percent of Total School Population)					
Low Income Rate	Limited English Proficient Rate	Chronic Truancy Rate	Mobility Rate	Attendance Rate	Total Enrollment
54	9	10	15	91	345

Parental contacts (includes parent–teacher conferences, parent visits to school, home visits, telephone conferences, and written correspondence) Percent: 81.4

Average Class Size (Sept. 15)			
Kindergarten	First	Second	Third
22.5	24.1	26.5	26.8

Minutes per Day Spent Teaching Reading			
Kindergarten	First	Second	Third
80	86	85	55

As we reviewed and discussed this data, I noted our high attendance rate given that a little over half of our student population was described as low income. The other information I noted was the teacher-reported information on how much time was spent teaching reading on average each day. I reflected on a university graduate course I recently completed on reading and remembered that research suggested that time spent on core reading activities each day should be at least 75 to 90 minutes. I wondered why the third-grade teachers indicated 55 minutes per day was spent on core reading activities. The next part of the State School Report Card listed results of the State Reading Proficiency Test. This test was administered to all students in each grade level each spring.

TABLE B: CASE 6.1   State Basic Reading Proficiency Test

Note: Percentages of student scores in the following four levels are indicated for each grade level.

Level 1—*Far below standards:* The student has very limited knowledge and skill in reading and is unable to apply reading effectively.

Level 2—*Below standards:* The student has basic knowledge and skill in reading and inconsistently applies reading effectively.

Level 3—*Meets standards:* The student has proficient basic knowledge and skill in reading and consistently applies reading effectively.

Level 4—*Exceeds standards:* The student has advanced knowledge and skill in reading and effectively applies reading.

	All Students			
Grade	**Level 1**	**Level 2**	**Level 3**	**Level 4**
Kindergarten	2	10	65	23
First grade	3	9	82	6
Second grade	5	9	81	5
Third grade	15	19	63	3

	Students with Disabilities			
Grade	**Level 1**	**Level 2**	**Level 3**	**Level 4**
Kindergarten	15	41	31	13
First grade	14	42	33	11
Second grade	15	44	29	12
Third grade	30	50	15	5

	Economically Disadvantaged			
Grade	**Level 1**	**Level 2**	**Level 3**	**Level 4**
Kindergarten	3	11	67	19
First grade	4	8	85	3
Second grade	4	10	83	3
Third grade	15	14	63	8

TABLE C: CASE 6.1   State Value-Added Assessment for Reading

Note: The value-added assessment results in a rating show the progress the school made in reading with students since the past school year. "Above" indicates that more than 1 year of progress was apparent and that students grew as expected. "Met" indicates that 1 year of progress was apparent and that students grew as expected. "Below" indicates that less than 1 year of progress was apparent and that students grew below the expected level.

Kindergarten—Section 1	Kindergarten—Section 2	Kindergarten—Section 3
Met	Met	Met
First Grade—Section 1	**First Grade—Section 2**	**First Grade—Section 3**
Met	Met	Met
Second Grade—Section 1	**Second Grade—Section 2**	**Second Grade—Section 3**
Met	Met	Below
Third Grade—Section 1	**Third Grade—Section 2**	**Third Grade—Section 3**
Below	Below	Below

It was interesting to note that the majority of our students in all grade levels met or exceeded reading standards. However, in third grade, 34% functioned below standards, compared with 12% to 14% in Grades K–2. The same pattern was apparent for students with disabilities. It also appeared that many students with disabilities did not meet reading standards across all grade levels. The vast majority of students who were economically disadvantaged met or exceeded reading standards. The next part of the State School Report Card summarized a new feature, student growth over 1 year.

From these results, it appeared that most students in each grade-level section showed 1 year of reading progress. The exception was third grade, where students in each section showed less than 1 year of progress. Next, the number of special education referrals was summarized.

It was clear that the majority of special education referrals were processed in third grade. I began to wonder about third grade. It wasn't clear what was happening, but the data we discussed seemed to indicate issues of concern in third grade.

TABLE D: CASE 6.1   Number of Special Education Referrals

Kindergarten—Section 1	Kindergarten—Section 2	Kindergarten—Section 3
0	0	2
First Grade—Section 1	**First Grade—Section 2**	**First Grade—Section 3**
3	1	2
Second Grade—Section 1	**Second Grade—Section 2**	**Second Grade—Section 3**
2	2	0
Third Grade—Section 1	**Third Grade—Section 2**	**Third Grade—Section 3**
6	8	10

Questions

1. What does this assessment data tell you about Marsh Elementary School?
2. Describe the strengths of the school, based on the information in the case.
3. As a member of this leadership team and based on this data, what would be the areas to focus on for improvement during the next school year?
4. What additional schoolwide assessment information could RtI provide to this leadership team?

CASE 6.2

The Future of Teaching

Background

Mr. Smith, the building principal, talked with me today about my third-year teaching evaluation. He reviewed his direct observation of my teaching and was very complimentary. He said that I motivated students, had excellent classroom discipline, and that I communicated well with the students. However, he also reviewed student outcome assessment data for students in my classroom and expressed concern. He indicated that some of my students were not meeting expected performance levels, based on the State Outcome Test. He told me that I would have to find the source of the problem and increase student scores or this could jeopardize my employment in the district. I have been teaching third-grade reading for 3 years in a school that recently implemented RtI. My students typically meet all standards on the state assessment. I was shocked!

(*Note to the reader:* There are two possible endings for this case. Read each and then answer the questions that follow.)

Scenario 1

One of my colleagues and my mentor, Juanita Rodriguiz, was a member of the school leadership team. She functioned as the data specialist for RtI implementation. I asked for assistance from Juanita to help me analyze available assessment data in an attempt to find the reason why student performance dropped. The first step was to look at the third-grade curriculum to ensure that it was aligned with the state standards. The RtI leadership team, along with classroom teachers, already determined that the curriculum was research based and aligned with the appropriate standards. Juanita agreed to review a sample of my lesson plans to ensure that I was implementing the curriculum with integrity. Juanita helped me schedule regular screening assessments for all students in my classroom. Students not meeting with success were part of a Tier 2 small-group supplemental intervention group. This group was scheduled to work with me three times a week for 25 minutes each session using a commercial research-supported program emphasizing phonics, comprehension, and vocabulary. The program was implemented with integrity, and student progress was monitored every other week. Juanita helped me with each step during the implementation of RtI. At the end of the semester, I saw from the progress-monitoring data that students in Tier 2 were making progress. In fact, by March, several students moved to Tier 1 from Tier 2.

In October, I met again with Mr. Smith to discuss my annual teaching evaluation. Again, he was complimentary about the classroom observation. I talked with him about the efforts I had made, using RtI, to improve student outcomes. I was able to show him how students had progressed, using screening results for all students and progress monitoring of individual students. Mr. Smith recommended my continued employment, in part because I was able to show student success. Without the help from Juanita and implementing RtI, I may have lost my job.

Scenario 2

I had no idea what to do. I talked with my colleague and mentor, James Johnson, the reading specialist. He suggested that I observe another third-grade teacher in the classroom. I observed, took notes, interviewed the teacher, and tried to implement new teaching strategies. I felt that my students came to me without a solid foundation in reading and that I simply could not reach everyone. However, I taught the core reading curriculum as well as I could. Everyone received the same instruction, and I noticed that five or six students seemed to struggle. After I made these observations, I tried to create extra reading activities for these students. I let them work on a computer program in reading or I gave them extra phonics worksheets. Occasionally, I listened to them read aloud from our reading text. I hoped that my extra efforts helped these struggling students. Although I didn't work with the smaller group regularly, every time there was a free moment, I tried to give them extra practice in reading.

In October, I met again with Mr. Smith about my teaching evaluation. I talked with him about the efforts I had made to improve my teaching. I wasn't completely sure that students had made progress, but I felt that they had improved. Mr. Smith talked with me about the State Outcome Test, and, again, students did not meet the standards. Mr. Smith was very discouraged as he told me I had one more year to determine what to do or I would not be recommended for continued employment.

Questions

1. Describe what the teacher did in Scenario 1 to address Mr. Smith's concerns.
2. Describe what the teacher did in Scenario 2 to address Mr. Smith's concerns.
3. How did the teacher's actions in each scenario differ?
4. If you were the teacher in this position, what would you do?

APPENDIX A

Assessment Example: How to Administer Teacher-Constructed Curriculum-Based Measurement Probes

Curriculum-based measurement (CBM) in reading is a procedure for monitoring student growth (Deno, 1985) that has been well-researched and generally regarded as reliable and valid (Waymann et al., 2007). Before using this option, review the following chart to determine if this assessment is a "good fit" for the assessment situation.

Description of assessment	Purpose of assessment	Appropriate for these grade levels	Teacher resources needed	Approximate time needed to prepare materials
Oral reading fluency—the student orally reads a written selection as the teacher counts the number of words read correctly	Progress monitoring	Second grade and above	Access to Internet; access to copying or printing; access to grade-level core reading curriculum	4–5 hours (does not include practicing and learning to administer the assessment)

The following steps can be used to organize and administer CBM in reading. The steps are adapted from Scott and Weishaar (2003).

Step 1: Collect 20 to 25 random samples of approximately 150 words for first and second grades and 250 words for third grade and up from the core reading curriculum textbooks. The teacher will need three samples to establish a baseline and one sample for the student to read every other week during progress monitoring (total of 20 to 25 samples). The samples should include narrative writing, not poetry or plays. Samples should not be too difficult for the child to read aloud (i.e., the student should be able to read approximately 85% of the words in a passage). One way to make sure that passages are not written above grade level is to calculate the readability of each passage. An easy way to estimate readability is to utilize the Flesch-Kinkaid readability estimate, which can be used as a tool in Microsoft Word. The method for applying this readability format will vary depending on the version of Word used. Generally, once in Word, utilize the Help menu to search "Display readability statistics." Information on the Flesch-Kinkaid readability formula is available online at http://www.readabilityformulas.com/flesch-reading-ease-readability-formula.php.

If the Flesch-Kinkaid readability statistics using Microsoft Word is not available, the Fry Readability Graph (Fry, 1977) can be used. This easy-to-use method of estimating readability is available in standard teacher education reading texts or online at http://www.readabilityformulas.com/fry-graph-readability-formula.php.

If the readability shows that the passages are consistently two or three grade levels above the student's current grade level, implementing CBM using the core curriculum textbooks may not be appropriate. It is important to note that the readability statistic is a broad estimate of the difficulty level of the passage. If the passage is too difficult for the student, it might be necessary to select passages from core curriculum materials at a lower grade level, keeping in mind that the number of words read correctly represents the student's skill in reading materials at a lower grade level.

Step 2: Retype the passages as indicated in the examples in Figures A.1 and A.2. The teacher will need two copies: one for the teacher to mark the number of words read correctly and the other for the student to read, which can be reused.

As an alternative to creating forms for the probes, the Web site Intervention Central houses the Curriculum-Based Measurement Warehouse, where teachers can create and download probes for their core curriculum to use for screening and progress monitoring in the area of reading. In addition, the Web site will automatically check the readability level of each probe. To use this option, go to CBM Warehouse using the following link: http://www.interventioncentral.org.

Step 3: Organize the passages. Student passages should be kept in a notebook and labeled. These can be reused. Teacher copies should be duplicated and organized in folders for easy access.

Student Name:_____ Date:_____	
Passage	**Cumulative Word Count**
One day after school, Paul walked down the street and met his	12
friend Sam. Paul and Sam decided that they were going to build	24
a tree house in the woods. They went to Paul's garage and found	37
some old pieces of wood, a saw, and some other tools. They dragged	50
an extension ladder out in the woods to a big tree. Paul placed the	64
ladder up against the tree and climbed up onto a branch. Sam held the	78
ladder as Paul climbed on the branch carrying a rope. Paul dropped the	91
rope down to Sam so that he could haul up the tools needed to build	106
the tree house. They boys used two-by-fours to build the frame for their tree	120
house. They hauled up sheets of plywood for the floor and sides of their	134
tree house. While they were working, it began to rain. They left their	147
tools in the woods and ran home.	154

Approximately readability of passage: 1.0

Number of words read in 1 minute: _____

Minus errors: _____

Score: _____

FIGURE A.1   Example: Teacher copy of Core Reading Passage

One day after school, Paul walked down the street and met his friend Sam. Paul and Sam decided that they were going to build a tree house in the woods. They went to Paul's garage and found some old pieces of wood, a saw, and some other tools. They dragged an extension ladder out in the woods to a big tree. Paul placed the ladder up against the tree and climbed up onto a branch. Sam held the ladder as Paul climbed on the branch carrying a rope. Paul dropped the rope down to Sam so that he could haul up the tools needed to build the tree house. These boys used two-by-fours to build the frame for their tree house. They hauled up sheets of plywood for the floor and sides of their tree house. While they were working, it began to rain. They left their tools in the woods and ran home.

FIGURE A.2   Example: Student Copy of Core Reading Passage

Step 4: Create graphs for each student whose progress will be monitored. Using regular graph paper, label the vertical axis as the number of words read correctly. Label the horizontal axis as the date that each probe was administered. Figure A.3 shows how the graph should be organized. Again, the Web site described under Step 2, Intervention Central (ChartDog) will automatically make graphs for your students.

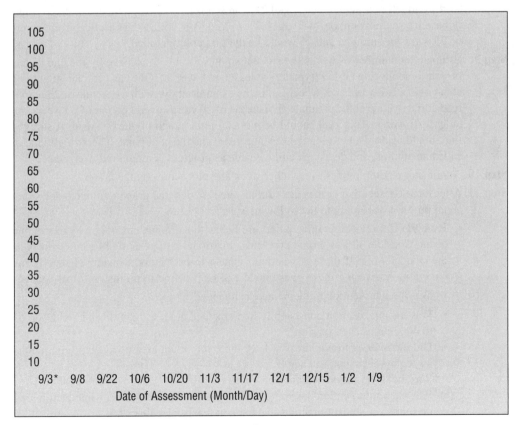

FIGURE A.3   Number of Words Read Correctly
*Baseline = Three probes with scores averaged

Step 5: Administer the reading probe using standard instructions. Tindal and Marston (1990) used the following instructions:

> When I say "start," begin reading at the top of this page. If you wait on a word too long, I'll tell you the word. If you come to a word you cannot read, just say "pass" and go on to the next word. Do not attempt to read as fast as you can. This is not a speed reading test. Read at a comfortable rate. At the end of 1 minute, I'll say "stop" (p. 148).

Step 6: Record errors as the student reads aloud as the teacher times 1 minute. As the student reads, make a slash mark (/) through any word read incorrectly. Incorrect words include words pronounced by the teacher, words the student does not attempt or says "pass," words mispronounced, words omitted, words that are read out of order, and words substituted for the correct word. After 1 minute, tell the student to stop reading and place a slash where the student stops.

Step 7: Write the number of words tried to read at the bottom of the teacher copy and subtract the number of words with slash marks or errors. The overall score will be the number of words attempted minus errors. The score, or number of words read correctly, is marked as a point on the graph.

Step 8: For three passages, administered over three different days, average the scores as the baseline score. For example, if the student read 24 words correctly on September 5, 30 words correctly on September 8, and 21 words correctly on September 10, the average or baseline score would be $24 + 30 + 21 = 75 \div 3 = 25$. So the baseline score would be 25 words per minute, and 25 would be the first point graphed.

Step 9: Estimate the number of words the student should be able to achieve by the end of the progress-monitoring period (typically at least 6 to 8 weeks). One can estimate growth of about one or two words per week. Using the example above with a baseline of 25 words read correctly, one could estimate an increase of 20 words over a period of 20 weeks, or at least 45 words. This goal should be plotted on the graph on the last date. A straight line should be drawn between the baseline score and the goal point. This straight line is called an aimline, and decisions will be made as progress is monitored over time.

Step 10: Administer reading probes every other week and plot scores on the graph.

Step 11: After three consecutive probes are administered, review the graph and make decisions about progress according to the following rules.

- **Rule #1:** If three consecutive points are below the aimline, consider why this might occur. Consider illness, home problems, emotional issues, or significant changes in the student's life. If these issues don't appear to be factors, consider change in instruction. Answering these questions could help define to an instructional change.
    - Was the intervention implemented as intended?
    - Was the intervention consistently implemented at least three times a week for 20 to 40 minutes each session?
    - Did the intervention address at least three important area of reading (e.g., phonics, comprehension, fluency)?
    - Was the intervention evidence based?
    - Was each intervention session characterized by student–teacher interaction, opportunity for student practice, and explicit teacher feedback?

        If the answers to these questions are affirmative, an instructional change could be warranted and might include intensifying the intervention (more time) or changing the intervention. If ongoing progress monitoring continues to show three more con-secutive data points below the aimline despite adjustments to instruction, consider Tier 3 intervention and referral to a building team.

- **Rule #2:** If three consecutive points are neither consistently above nor below the aimline, don't make changes. For example, if one point is above and the next two consecutive points are below the aimline, no changes are needed. Continue to apply the intervention and monitor student progress.

- **Rule #3:** If three consecutive points are above the aimline, consider returning the student to Tier 1 for instruction. Before making this change, however, determine how far away the student score is from the expected benchmark. If the student score is far away from the benchmark score, moving the student to Tier 1 would not be a good idea. However, if the student appears to be close to the benchmark score, this might be the best option. In this case, progress monitoring might be discontinued, and the student would participate in regular screening.

APPENDIX B

Assessment Example: How to Administer and Organize the Dynamic Indicators of Early Basic Literacy Skills (DIBELS)

Dynamic Indicators of Early Basic Literacy Skills (DIBELS; University of Oregon) represents a valid, reliable, research-based, efficient, and low-cost tool for screening and monitoring progress that directly relates to the important areas of early reading (Student Progress Monitoring, 2007). Before implementing this option, review the following chart to determine if this assessment is a good fit for the assessment situation.

Description of assessment	Purpose of assessment	Appropriate for these grade levels	Teacher resources needed	Approximate time needed to prepare materials
Early reading skills (initial sound fluency, phonemic segmentation fluency, nonsense word fluency)	Screening and progress monitoring	Kindergarten and first grade	Access to Internet; access to copying or printing	1 hour per assessment (does not include practicing and learning to administer the assessment)
Oral reading fluency	Screening and progress monitoring	Second grade and above		

OVERVIEW

For kindergarten and first grade, three assessments are suggested. These assessments may be used for screening and monitoring progress. For Grades 2–6, one assessment is used for both screening and monitoring progress. Kindergarten measures are summarized in Table B.1, first-grade assessments are summarized in Table B.2, and second- through sixth-grade assessments are summarized in Table B.3.

TABLE B.1   Kindergarten Assessment

DIBELS assessment	Description of kindergarten assessment	Estimated time to prepare materials (Download and copy)	Estimated time to read materials and learn how to administer (Including assessment integrity checklist)*	Estimated time to administer assessment
Initial sound fluency	When shown a set of pictures, the student is asked to identify the picture that begins with a particular phoneme.	Approximately 1 hour	Approximately 1 hour	4–5 minutes per child
Phonemic segmentation fluency	After the teacher says a word, the student tells the phonemes in the word (cat = c/a/t).	Approximately 1 hour	Approximately 1 hour	4–5 minutes per child
Nonsense word fluency	The student is asked to correctly identify as many nonsense words as possible in 1 minute given a list of words.	Approximately 1 hour	Approximately 1 hour	4–5 minutes per child

*Not including time to practice administration

TABLE B.2   First-Grade Assessment

DIBELS assessment	Description of first grade assessment	Estimated time to prepare materials (Download and copy)	Estimated time to read materials and learn how to administer (Including assessment integrity checklist)*	Estimated time to administer assessment
Phonemic segmentation fluency	After the teacher says a word, the student tells the phonemes in the word (cat = c/a/t).	Approximately 1 hour	Approximately 1 hour	4–5 minutes per child
Nonsense word fluency	The student is asked to correctly identify as many nonsense words as possible in 1 minute given a list of words.	Approximately 1 hour	Approximately 1 hour	4–5 minutes per child
DIBELS oral reading fluency	The student reads aloud a selection for 1 minute and the teacher counts the number of words read correctly and incorrectly.	Approximately 1 hour	Approximately 1 hour	4–5 minutes per child

*Not including time to practice administration

TABLE B.3   Second- Through Sixth-Grade Assessment

DIBELS assessment	Description of second through sixth grade assessment	Estimated time to prepare materials (Download and copy)	Estimated time to read materials and understand how to administer (Including assessment integrity checklist)*	Estimated time to administer assessment
DIBELS oral reading fluency	The student reads aloud a selection for 1 minute and the teacher counts the number of words read correctly and incorrectly.	Approximately 1 hour	Approximately 1 hour	4–5 minutes per child

*Not including time to practice administration

HOW TO ORGANIZE AND ADMINISTER DIBELS

Step 1: Log on to this Web site: https://dibels.uoregon.edu/measures/

Step 2: Sign up for a free account.

Step 3: Download and print appropriate materials in the following list. Please note that both screening and progress-monitoring materials will be downloaded and printed. Progress monitoring is discussed in Chapter 4.

Kindergarten materials include the following:

- Administration and Scoring Guide and any supplemental scoring information. (Good & Kaminski, 2002)
- Kindergarten Scoring Booklet (for screening) (Good & Kaminski, 2007a)
- Phonemic Segmentation Fluency Progress Monitoring Kindergarten Scoring Booklet (Good, Kaminski, & Smith, 2007)
- Initial Sound Fluency Progress Monitoring Kindergarten Scoring Booklet (Good, Laimon, Kaminski, & Smith, 2007)

First-grade materials include the following:

- Administration and Scoring Guide and any supplemental scoring information (Good & Kaminski, 2002)
- First Grade Scoring Booklet Benchmark Assessment (for screening) (Good & Kaminski, 2007c)
- Phonemic Segmentation Fluency Progress Monitoring Kindergarten Scoring Booklet (Good, Kaminski, & Smith, 2007)
- Nonsense Word Fluency Progress Monitoring First Grade Scoring Booklet (Good & Kaminski, 2007k)
- Oral Reading Fluency Progress Monitoring First Grade Student Materials (Good, Kaminski, & Dill, 2007c)

Second- through sixth-grade materials include the following:

- Administration and Scoring Guide and any supplemental scoring information (Good & Kaminski, 2002)

- Appropriate level (second through sixth) Grade Scoring Booklet Benchmark Assessment (for screening) (Good & Kaminski, 2007b, d, e, f, g)

- Appropriate level (second through sixth) Grade Oral Reading Fluency Progress Monitoring Student Materials (Good & Kaminski, 2007h, i, j, l, m; Good, Kaminski, & Dill, 2007)

Step 4: Organize and copy the appropriate grade-level Scoring Booklet Benchmark Assessment (used for screening).

- Make one copy of the student response form for each student. Assemble the booklets.

- Place the student reusable stimulus materials in a notebook, labeling the notebook—e.g., "Screening—Kindergarten," "Screening—First Grade," "Screening—Second Grade" (or Third Grade, Fourth Grade, Sixth Grade).

Step 5: Organize and copy progress-monitoring booklets (as discussed in Chapter 4).

- For each assessment, make one copy of the student response form for each student and assemble the booklets.

- Place the student reusable stimulus materials in separate notebooks, labeling each "Progress Monitoring."

- For kindergarten, the notebooks would be labeled "Progress Monitoring—Phoneme Segmentation Fluency—Kindergarten," and "Progress Monitoring—Initial Sound Fluency—Kindergarten."

- For first grade, they would be labeled "Progress Monitoring—Phoneme Segmentation Fluency," "Progress Monitoring—Nonsense Word Fluency," and "Progress Monitoring—Oral Reading Fluency."

- For second through sixth grades, the notebooks would be labeled "Progress Monitoring—Oral Reading Fluency."

Step 6: Thoroughly read the Administration and Scoring Guide and supplemental scoring information. Also read the directions for progress monitoring in the student response form for each assessment. (*Note:* These are short-form directions that were already read in the Administration and Scoring Guide.)

Step 7: Find an adult partner (preferably someone who is familiar with assessment, like another teacher, school psychologist, speech therapist, etc.) who is willing to play the part of a kindergarten student. Practice administering the screening assessments and then the progress-monitoring assessments, paying special attention to following the procedures and directions *exactly* as they are stated. Practice at least 10 times or until completely comfortable administering all assessments.

Step 8: Ask the partner to observe practice administration of the screening assessments and then the progress-monitoring assessments to a student. The observing partner should use a copy of the Assessment Integrity Checklist (located in the Administration and Scoring Guide) as he or she observes administration of each assessment. There is a separate Assessment Integrity Checklist for each assessment. As each assessment is administered, the partner checks each item to indicate if the teacher is proficient or needs additional practice with the assessment. After each assessment, the partner should review the checklist with the teacher. If additional practice is needed, Steps 7 and 8 should be repeated until this checklist is "passed"—i.e., all items on the checklist are listed as proficient.

REFERENCES

American Institutes for Research, National Center on Response to Intervention. (2009, April). *Glossary of RTI terms*. Retrieved April 4, 2009, from: http://www.rti4success.org/index.php?option=com_content&task=view&id=1132&Itemid=142#ProgressMonitoring

American Institutes for Research, National Center on Response to Intervention. (2009, June 5). *Progress monitoring tools chart: Reading and math*. Retrieved June 5, 2009, from: http://www.rti4success.org/chart/progressMonitoring/progressmonitoringtoolschart.htm#

Association for Childhood Education International. (2007). *Elementary education standards and supporting explanation*. Retrieved July 8, 2009, from: http://www.ncate.org/ProgramStandards/ACEI/ACEIscoringGuide_07.doc

Baker, S. K., Plasencia-Peinado, J., & Lozcano-Lytle, V. (1998). The use of curriculum-based measurement with language-minority students. In M. R. Shinn (Ed.), *Advanced applications of curriculum-based measurement* (pp. 175–213). New York: Guilford Press.

Batsche, G. (2006). *Problem-solving and response to intervention: Implications for state and district policies and practice* [PowerPoint slides]. Retrieved October 6, 2008, from: http://www.casecec.org/powerpoints/rti/CASE%20Dr.%20George%20Batsche%201—25-2006.ppt

Batsche, G. (n.d.). *Building support*. RTI Action Network. Retrieved March 25, 2010, from: http://www.rtinetwork.org/GetStarted/BuildSupport/ar/BuildingSupport

Batsche, G. M., Elliott, J., Graden, J., Grimes, J. Kovaleski, F. F., Prasse, D., et al. (2005). *Response to Intervention: Policy considerations and implementation*. Alexandria, VA: National Association of State Directors of Special Education, Inc.

Becvar, R., & Becvar, D. (1982). *Systems theory and family therapy*. Washington, DC: University Press of America.

Board of Education of the Hendrick Hudson Central School District v. Rowlet, 458 U.S. 176 (1982).

Brigance, A. H. (1999). *BRIGANCE diagnostic comprehensive inventory of basic skills, revised*. North Billerica, MA: Curriculum Associates.

Chaney, P. F. (2008). *Incorporating student progress monitoring in teacher education courses* [PowerPoint slides]. Retrieved September 9, 2009, from: http://www.studentprogress.org/doc/TeacherEdWebinar.ppt#257

Clay, M. M. (2000). *Running records for classroom teachers*. Portsmouth, NH: Heinemann.

Council of Chief State School Officers. (1992). *Interstate New Teacher Assessment and Support Consortium: Model standards for beginning teacher licensing, assessment and development*. Retrieved September 25, 2009, from: http://www.ccsso.org/content/pdfs/corestrd.pdf

Council of Chief State School Officers' Interstate Teacher Assessment and Support Consortium. (2010). *Model core teaching standards: A resource for state dialogue*. Retrieved September 14, 2010, from: http://www.ccsso.org/Documents/2010/Model_Core_Teaching_Standards_DRAFT_FOR_PUBLIC_COMMENT_2010.pdf

Deno, S. L. (1985). Curriculum-based measurement: The emerging alternative. *Exceptional Children, 52*, 219–232.

Deno, S. L. (2003). Developments in curriculum-based measurement. *Journal of Special Education, 37*, 184–192.

Deno, S. L., & Fuchs, L. S. (1987). Developing curriculum-based measurement systems for data-based special education problem solving. *Focus on Exceptional Children, 19*(8), 1–15.

Deno, S., Lembke, E., & Reschly Anderson, A. (n.d.). *Progress monitoring: Study group content module*. Retrieved October 20, 2008, from http://www.progress-monitoring.org/pdf/cbmMOD1.pdf

Denton, C. A., Vaughn, S., & Fletcher, J. M. (2003). Bring research-based practice in reading intervention to scale. *Learning Disabilities Research and Practice, 18*, 201–211.

Elliott, J. (2008). Response to intervention: What & why? *School Administrator, 65*(8), 10–18.

Elliott, J., & Morrison, D. (2008). *Response to intervention blueprints: District level edition*. Alexandria, VA: National Association of State Directors of Special Education.

Evergreen Freedom Foundation (2001). *School directors' handbook*. Retrieved April 19, 2010, from http://www.effwa.org/studies/sdh.php

Florida Center for Reading Research. (n.d.-a). *FCRR reports*. Retrieved April 15, 2009, from http://www.fcrr.org/FCRRReports/reportslist.htm

Florida Center for Reading Research. (n.d.-b). *Principal reading walk-through checklists.* Retrieved April 15, 2009, from http://www.fcrr.org/Curriculum/curriculum.htm

Fry, E. (1977). Fry's readability graph: Clarification, validity and extensions to level 17. *Journal of Reading, 21,* 242–252.

Fuchs, L. S. (2007a). *NRCLD update on responsiveness to intervention: Research to practice* [Brochure]. Lawrence, KS: National Research Center on Learning Disabilities.

Fuchs, L. S. (2007b). *Monitoring student progress in the classroom to enhance teaching, planning, and student learning* [PowerPoint slides]. Retrieved October 30, 2009, from http://www.studentprogress.org/doc/webinars/DrLynnFuchsPresentationslides.pdf

Fuchs, D., & Deshler, D. D. (2007). What we need to know about responsiveness to intervention (and shouldn't be afraid to ask). *Learning Disabilities Research & Practice, 22*(2), 129–136.

Fuchs, L. S., & Fuchs, D. (1999). Monitoring student progress toward the development of reading competence: A review of three forms of classroom-based assessment. *School Psychology Review, 28*(4), 659–671.

Fuchs, L. S., & Fuch, D. (2006). Implementing responsiveness-to-intervention to identify learning disabilities. *Perspectives on Dyslexia, 32*(1), 39–43.

Fuchs, L. S., & Fuchs, D. (2007). *Progress monitoring in the context of responsiveness-to-intervention.* Retrieved November 11, 2008, from http://www.studentprogress.org/summer_institute/2007/RTI/RTIManual2007.pdf

Fuchs, L. S., & Fuchs, D. (n.d.). *Using CBM for progress monitoring in reading.* Retrieved October 24, 2008, from http://www.studentprogress.org/summer_institute/2007/Intro%20reading/IntroReading_Manual_2007.pdf

Fuchs, L. S., Fuchs, D., Hosp, M., & Jenkins, J. R. (2001). Oral reading fluency as an indicator of reading competence: A theoretical, empirical, and historical analysis. *Scientific Studies of Reading, 5,* 239–256.

Fuchs, L. S., Fuchs, D., & Zumeta, R. O. (2008). Response to intervention: A strategy for the prevention and identification of learning disabilities. In E. L. Grigorenko (Ed.), *Educating individuals with disabilities: IDEIA 2004 and beyond.* New York: Springer.

Gersten, R., Baker, S. K., Shanahan, T., Linan-Thompson, S., Collins, P., & Scarcella, R. (2007). *Effective literacy and English language instruction for English learners in the elementary grades: A practice guide* (CEE 2007-4011). Washington, DC: National Center for Education Evaluation and Regional Assistance, Institute of Education Sciences, U.S. Department of Education. Retrieved September 16, 2009, from http://ies.ed.gov/ncee.

Gersten, R., Compton, D., Connor, C. M., Dimino, J., Santory, L., Linan-Thompson, S., & Tilly, W. D. (2009). *Assisting students struggling with reading: Response to Intervention and multi-tier intervention for reading in the primary grades. A practice guide.* (NCEE 2009-4045). Washington, DC: National Center for Education Evaluation and Regional Assistance, Institute of Education Sciences, U.S. Department of Education. Retrieved September 20, 2009, from http://ies.ed.gov/ncee/wwc/publications/practiceguides/

Good, R. H., & Kaminski, R. A. (Eds.). (2002). *Dynamic indicators of basic early literacy skills* (6th ed.). *Administration and scoring guide.* Eugene, OR: Institute for the Development of Educational Achievement. Retrieved August 13, 2009, from http://dibels.uoregon.edu/

Good, R. H., & Kaminski, R. A. (Eds.). (2007a). *Dynamic indicators of basic early literacy skills* (6th ed.). *kindergarten scoring booklet DIBELS benchmark assessment.* Eugene, OR: Institute for the Development of Educational Achievement. Retrieved August 13, 2009, from http://dibels.uoregon.edu/

Good, R. H., & Kaminski, R. A. (Eds.). (2007b). *Dynamic indicators of basic early literacy skills* (6th ed.). *Fifth grade scoring booklet DIBELS benchmark assessment.* Eugene, OR: Institute for the Development of Educational Achievement. Retrieved August 13, 2009, from http://dibels.uoregon.edu/

Good, R. H., & Kaminski, R. A. (Eds.). (2007c). *Dynamic indicators of basic early literacy skills* (6th ed.). *First grade scoring booklet DIBELS benchmark assessment.* Eugene, OR: Institute for the Development of Educational Achievement. Retrieved August 13, 2009, from http://dibels.uoregon.edu/

Good, R. H., & Kaminski, R. A. (Eds.). (2007d). *Dynamic indicators of basic early literacy skills* (6th ed.). *Fourth grade scoring booklet DIBELS benchmark assessment.* Eugene, OR: Institute for the Development of Educational Achievement. Retrieved August 13, 2009, from http://dibels.uoregon.edu/

Good, R. H., & Kaminski, R. A. (Eds.). (2007e). *Dynamic indicators of basic early literacy skills* (6th ed.). *Second* grade scoring booklet DIBELS benchmark assessment. Eugene, OR: Institute for the Development of Educational Achievement. Retrieved August 13, 2009, from http://dibels.uoregon.edu/

Good, R. H., & Kaminski, R. A. (Eds.). (2007f). *Dynamic indicators of basic early literacy skills* (6th ed.). *Sixth grade scoring booklet DIBELS benchmark assessment.* Eugene, OR: Institute for the Development of Educational Achievement. Retrieved August 13, 2009, from http://dibels.uoregon.edu/

Good, R. H., & Kaminski, R. A. (Eds.). (2007g). *Dynamic indicators of basic early literacy skills* (6th ed.). *Third grade scoring booklet DIBELS benchmark assessment.* Eugene, OR: Institute for the Development of Educational Achievement. Retrieved August 13, 2009, from http://dibels.uoregon.edu/

Good, R. H., & Kaminski, R. A. (Eds.). (2007h). *Dynamic indicators of basic literacy skills* (6th ed.). *DIBELS Oral reading fluency progress monitoring fifth grade scoring booklet.* Eugene, OR: Institute for the Development of Educational Achievement. Retrieved August 13, 2009, from http://dibels.uoregon.edu/

Good, R. H., & Kaminski, R. A. (Eds.). (2007i). *Dynamic indicators of basic literacy skills* (6th ed.). *DIBELS oral reading fluency progress monitoring fourth grade scoring booklet.* Eugene, OR: Institute for the Development of Educational Achievement. Retrieved August 13, 2009, from http://dibels.uoregon.edu/

Good, R. H., & Kaminski, R. A. (Eds.). (2007j). *Dynamic indicators of basic literacy skills* (6th ed.). *DIBELS oral reading fluency progress monitoring sixth grade scoring booklet.* Eugene, OR: Institute for the Development of Educational Achievement. Retrieved August 13, 2009, from http://dibels.uoregon.edu/

Good, R. H., & Kaminski, R. A. (2007k). Nonsense word fluency. In R. H. Good & R. A. Kaminski (Eds.), *Dynamic indicators of basic early literacy skills* (6th ed.). *DIBELS Nonsense word fluency progress monitoring first grade scoring booklet.* Eugene, OR: Institute for the Development of Educational Achievement. Retrieved August 13, 2009, from http://dibels.uoregon.edu/

Good, R. H., Kaminski, R. A., & Dill, S. (2007a). DIBELS oral reading fluency. In R. H. Good & R. A. Kaminski (Eds.), *Dynamic indicators of basic early literacy skills* (6th ed.) *DIBELS oral reading fluency progress monitoring second grade scoring booklet.* Eugene, OR: Institute for the Development of Educational

Achievement. Retrieved August 13, 2009, from http://dibels.uoregon.edu/

Good, R. H., Kaminski, R. A., & Dill, S. (2007b). DIBELS oral reading fluency. In R. H. Good & R. A. Kaminski (Eds.), *Dynamic indicators of basic early literacy skills* (6th ed.). *DIBELS oral reading fluency progress monitoring third grade scoring booklet.* Eugene, OR: Institute for the Development of Educational Achievement. Retrieved August 13, 2009, from http://dibels.uoregon.edu/

Good, R. H. , Kaminski, R. A., & Dill, S. (2007c). DIBELS oral reading fluency. In R. H. Good & R. A. Kaminski (Eds.), *Dynamic indicators of basic early literacy skills* (6th ed.). *DIBELS oral reading fluency progress monitoring first grade student materials.* Eugene, OR: Institute for the Development of Educational Achievement. Retrieved August 13, 2009, from: http://dibels.uoregon.edu/

Good, R. H., Kaminski, R.A., & Smith, S. (2007). Phoneme segmentation fluency. In R. H. Good & R. A. Kaminski (Eds.), *Dynamic indicators of basic early literacy skills* (6th ed.). *DIBELS phoneme segmentation fluency progress monitoring kindergarten scoring booklet.* Eugene, OR: Institute for Development of Educational Achievement. Retrieved August 13, 2009, from http://dibels.uoregon.edu

Good, R. H., Laimon, D., Kaminski, R. A., & Smith, S. (2007). Initial sound fluency. In R. H. Good & R. A. Kaminski (Eds.), *Dynamic indicators of basic early literacy skills* (6th ed.). *DIBELS initial sound fluency progress monitoring kindergarten scoring booklet.* Eugene, OR: Institute for Development of Educational Achievement. Retrieved August 13, 2009, from http://dibels.uoregon.edu

Hamilton, L, Halverson, R., Jackson, S. S., Mandinach, E., Supovitz, J. A., & Wayman, J. C. (2009). *Using student achievement data to support instructional decision making: A practice guide* (NCEE 2009-4067). Washington, DC: National Center for Education Evaluation and Regional Assistance, Institute of Education Sciences, U.S. Department of Education. Retrieved September 20, 2009, from http://ies.ed.gov/ncee/wwc/publications/practiceguides/

Hershberg, T. (n.d.). *The Center for Greater Philadelphia: Operation public education, value added assessment.* Retrieved April 13, 2010, from http://www.cgp.upenn.edu/ope_value.html

Hintze, J. (2007). *Using student progress monitoring in a response to intervention model.* Retrieved October 21,

2008, from http://www.studentprogress.org/library/Webinars.asp#ABC

Hoover, J. J., Baca, L., Wexler-Love, E., & Saenz, L. (2008). *National implementation of response to intervention (RTI): Research summary.* Boulder, CO: BUENO Center-School of Education, University of Colorado.

Hosp, J. L. (n.d.). *Response to intervention and the disproportionate representation of culturally and linguistically diverse students in special education.* Retrieved March 10, 2010, from: http://www.rtinetwork.org/Learn?Diversity/ar/DisproportionateRepresentation

Hosp, M. K., & Hosp, J. (2003). Curriculum-based measurement for reading, math, and spelling: How to do it and why. *Preventing School Failure, 48*(1), 10–17.

Host, M. K. (2007). *The ABCs of progress monitoring in reading* [PowerPoint slides]. Retrieved November 15, 2009, from: http://www.studentprogress.org/doc/webinars/ABCsProgressMonitoringinReading.pdf

Illinois State Board of Education, Illinois ASPIRE. (n.d.-a). *Scientifically based progress monitoring in reading using curriculum-based measurement and early literacy measures in a 3-tiered model* [PowerPoint slides]. Retrieved October 28, 2008, from: http://www.illinoisaspire.org/welcome/Scientifically_Based_Progress_Monitoring.ppt#3

Illinois State Board of Education, Illinois ASPIRE. (n.d.-b). *Universal screening* [PowerPoint slides]. Retrieved October 17, 2008, from: http://www.illinoisaspire.org/welcome/Universal_Screening.ppt

Individuals with Disabilities Education Improvement Act. (2004). Retrieved October 7, 2009, from www.ed.gov/about/offices/list/osers/osep/index.html

Individuals with Disabilities Education Improvement Act Regulations, 34 C.F.R. § 300.307 (2006).

Individuals with Disabilities Education Improvement Act Regulations, 34 C.F.R. § 300.226 (a)–(b) (2006).

Jenkins, J. & Johnson, E. (n.d.). *Universal screening for reading problems: Why and how should we do this.* Retrieved October 22, 2008, from http://www.rtinetwork.org/Essential/Assessment/Universal/ar/ReadingProblems

Johnson, E., Mellard, D. F., Fuchs, D., & McKnight, M. A. (2006). *Responsiveness to intervention: How to do it.* Lawrence, KS: National Research Center on Learning Disabilities.

Kaminski, R. A., & Good, R. H. (1998). Assessing early literacy in a problem-solving model: Dynamic indicators of basic early literacy skills. In M. R. Shinn (Ed.), *Advanced applications of curriculum-based measurement* (pp. 113–142). New York: Guilford.

Klein, A. (2010, February 10). Education budget plan wielded as policy lever: Competition, streamlining key elements. *Education Week, 1*, 18–19.

Klein, A. (2010, March 31). Tests loom for ESEA in Congress. *Education Week, 1*, 22–23.

Klingner, J. K., & Edwards, P. A. (2006). Cultural considerations with response to intervention models. *Reading Research Quarterly, 41*(1), 108–117.

Kurns, S., & Tilly, W. D. (2008). *Response to Intervention blueprints: School building level.* Alexandria, VA: National Association of State Directors of Special Education.

Marshall, J. (2009). *Welcome to achievement today: Response to Intervention (RTI) adoption survey 2009.* Towson, MD: Spectrum K12, Council of Administrators of Special Education, National Association of State Directors of Special Education, and American Association of School Administrators. Retrieved June 2, 2009, from www.spectrumk12.com/rti_survey_results.

Mastropieri, M. A., & Scruggs, T. E. (2007). *The inclusive classroom: Strategies for effective instruction* (3rd ed.). Upper Saddle River, NJ: Merrill/Pearson.

McLoughlin, J. A., & Lewis, R. B. (2008). *Assessing students with special needs* (7th ed.). Upper Saddle River, NJ: Merrill/Pearson.

Mellard, D. F., & Johnson, E. (2008). *RTI: A practitioner's guide to implementing response to intervention.* Thousand Oaks, CA: Corwin Press.

Miller, J. (2007). *Administration and scoring of early literacy and oral reading fluency measures* [PowerPoint slides]. Retrieved October 16, 2008, from: http://www.ilispa.org/uploads/smartsection/48_JMiller__CMartin_Universal_Screening_and_Benchmarking_.ppt

National Association for the Education of Young Children. (2001). *NAEYC standards for early childhood professional preparation: Initial licensure programs.* Retrieved October 10, 2009, from http://www.naeyc.org/files/ncate/file/initiallicensure.pdf

National Association of State Boards of Education. (1992). *Winners all: A call for inclusive schools.* Alexandria, VA: Author.

National Association of State Directors of Special Education. (2006). *Response to Intervention: A joint* paper by the National Association of State Directors of Special Education and the Council of Administrators of Special Education [White paper]. Retrieved August 25, 2009, from http://www.nasdse.org/Portals/0/ Documents/Download%20Publications/ RtIAnAdministratorsPerspective1—06.pdf

National Board for Professional Teaching Standards. (n.d.). *What teachers should know and be able to do.* Retrieved September 25, 2009, from http://www. nbpts.org/UserFiles/File/what_teachers.pdf

National Commission on Excellence in Education (1983). *A nation at risk: The imperative for educational reform.* Washington, DC: U.S. Government Printing Office.

National Council for Accreditation of Teacher Education. (2008 February). *Professional standards for the accreditation of teacher preparation institutions.* Washington, DC: National Council for Accreditation of Teacher Education (NCATE).

National Council for Accreditation of Teacher Education/Council for Exceptional Children. (2002). *NCATE/CEC program standards (2002): Programs for the preparation of special education teachers.* Retrieved October 10, 2009, from http://www.ncate. org/ProgramStandards/CEC/CECStandards.doc

National Implementation Research Network. (2010). *Louis de la Parte, Florida Mental Health Institute, University of South Florida.* Retrieved on April 13, 2010, from http://www.fpg.unc.edu/~nirn/

National Institute of Child Health and Human Development. (2000, Spring). *Report of the National Reading Panel. Teaching children to read: An evidence-based assessment of the scientific research literature on reading and its implications for reading instruction* (NIH Publication No. 00–4769). Washington, DC: U.S. Government Printing Office.

National Research Center on Learning Disabilities. (2007a). *Responsiveness to intervention in the SLD determination process* [Brochure]. Lawrence, KS: Author.

National Research Center on Learning Disabilities. (2007b). *SLD identification overview: General information and tools to get started* [Brochure]. Lawrence, KS: Author.

National Research Council. (2002). *Executive summary: Disproportionate representation of minority students in special education.* Washington, DC: Author.

No Child Left Behind Act of 2001. Retrieved October 15, 2009, from http://www.ed.gov/policy/elsec/leg/esea02/

Operation Public Education. (n.d.). *New systems of assessment and accountability to transform America's schools.* Retrieved April 19, 2010, from http://www.cgp. upenn.edu/ope.html

Oregon Reading First Center. (n.d.). *List of the nine general features of instruction.* Retrieved April 15, 2009, from http://oregonreadingfirst.uoregon.edu/ inst_obs.html

Pierangelo, R., & Giuliani, G. (2008). *Frequently asked questions about Response to Intervention.* Thousand Oaks, CA: Corwin Press.

President's Commission on Special Education Excellence. (2002). *A new era: Revitalizing special education for all children and their families.* Washington, DC: U.S. Department of Education.

Rebora, A. (2010, April 12). Responding to RTI. *Education Week Teacher, 3*(2), 20.

Reschly, D. J., Holdheide, L. R., Smartt, S. M., & Oliver, R. M. (2008, June). *Evaluation of LBS-1 teacher preparation in inclusive practices, reading, and classroom organization-behavior management.* Springfield: Illinois State Board of Education.

Roe, B. D., & Burns, P. C. (2007). *Informal reading inventory* (7th ed.). Boston: Houghton Mifflin.

Sawchuk, S. (2010, March 10). Rules proposed for revamping teacher pay. *Education Week, 19,* 24.

Scott, F. G., & Weishaar, M. K. (2003). Curriculum-Based Measurement for reading progress. *Intervention in School and Clinic, 38*(3), 153–159.

Scott, V. G. (2009). *Phonemic awareness: Ready-to-use lessons, activities, and games* (2nd ed). Thousand Oaks, CA: Corwin Press.

Shinn, M. R. (2002). *AIMSweb Training Workbook: Organizing and implementing a benchmark assessment program.* Eden Prairie, MN: Edformation, Inc.

Shinn, M. M., & Shinn, M. R. (2002a). *AIMSweb Training Workbook: Administration and scoring of early literacy measures for use with AIMSweb.* Eden Prairie, MN: Edformation, Inc.

Shinn, M. M., & Shinn, M. R. (2002b). *AIMSweb Training Workbook: Administration and scoring of reading curriculum-based measurement (R-CBM) for use in general outcome measurement.* Eden Prairie, MN: Edformation, Inc.

Shinn, M. M., & Shinn, M. R. (2002c). *AIMSweb Training Workbook: Administration and scoring of reading maze for use in general outcome measurement*. Eden Prairie, MN: Edformation, Inc.

Shinn, M. R., Shinn, M. M., Hamilton, C., & Clarke, B. (2002). Using curriculum-based measurement to promote achievement in general education classrooms. In M.R. Shinn, G. Stoner & H.M. Walker (Eds.), *Interventions for academic and behavior problems: Preventative and remedial approaches* (pp. 113–142). Bethesda, MD: National Association of School Psychologists.

Shores, C., & Chester, K. (2009). *Using TTI for school improvement*. Thousand Oaks, CA: Corwin Press.

Silvaroli, N. J., & Wheelock, W. H. (2004). *Classroom reading inventory* (10th ed.). Boston: McGraw-Hill.

Simmons, D. C., Kame'enui, E. J., Good III, R. H., Harn, B., Cole, C., & Braun, D. (2002). Building, implementing, and sustaining a beginning reading improvement model: Lessons learned school by school. In M. R. Shinn, G. Stoner, & H. M. Walker (Eds.), *Interventions for academic and behavior problems: Preventive and remedial approaches*. Bethesda, MD: National Association of School Psychologists.

Smartt, S. M., & Reschly, D. J. (2007). *Barriers to the preparation of highly qualified teachers in reading*. Washington, DC: National Comprehensive Center for Teacher Quality. Retrieved September 23, 2009, from http://www.ncctq.org/publications/June2007Brief.pdf

Stecker, P. M., & Lembke, E. S. (2005). *Advanced applications of CBM in reading: Instructional decision-making strategies manual*. Washington, DC: US Office of Special Education Programs. Retrieved January 27, 2010, from http://www.studentprogress.org/library/Training/CBMmath/AdvancedReading/AdvRdgManual-FORMATTEDSept29.pdf

Student Progress Monitoring. (2007). [Review of Progress Monitoring Tools]. Retrieved October 19, 2009, from: http://www.studentprogress.org/chart/chart.asp

Tilly, W. D., Harken, S., Robinson, W., & Kurns, S. (2008). Three tiers of intervention, *The School Administrator*, *65*(8), 20–23.

Tindal, G. A., & Marston, D. B. (1990). *Classroom-based assessment*. New York: Merrill/Macmillan.

Turnbull, H. R., & Turnbull, A. P. (2000). *Free appropriate public education: The law and children with disabilities* (6th ed.). Denver, CO: Love Publishing Co.

University of Oregon Center on Teaching and Learning (2002–2008). *Big ideas in beginning reading*. Retrieved November 17, 2008, from http://reading.uoregon.edu/

University of Oregon Center on Teaching and Learning (n.d.). *DIBELS data system* [Materials downloads]. Retrieved November 17, 2008, from University of Oregon: https://dibels.uoregon.edu/measures/

University of Oregon Center on Teaching and Learning (n.d.). *Frequently asked questions: Progress monitoring*. Retrieved September 2, 2009, from University of Oregon: https://dibels.uoregon.edu/faq.php#faq_cat9

U.S. Department of Education. (2009). *Race to the Top program executive summary*. Retrieved March 10, 2010, from http://www2.ed.gov/programs/racetothetop/executive-summary.pdf.

U.S. Department of Education (March 2010). *A blueprint for reform: The reauthorization of the Elementary and Secondary Education Act*. Washington, DC: U.S. Department of Education, Office of Planning, Evaluation and Policy Development.

U.S. Department of Education, Institute of Education Sciences (n.d.). *What works clearinghouse*. Retrieved April 16, 2009, from http://ies.ed.gov/ncee/wwc/reports/

U.S. Department of Education, National Center for Education Statistics. (2009). *The Condition of Education 2009*. Washington, DC: Office of Educational Research and Improvement.

U.S. Department of Health and Human Services (2000). *Report of the National Reading Panel: Teaching children to read summary* (NIH Pub. No. 00–4769). Retrieved September 24, 2009, from National Institute of Child Health and Human Development: http://www.nichd.nih.gov/publications/nrp/smallbook.cfm

Walsh, K., Glaser, D. R., & Wilcox, D. D. (2006). *What education schools aren't teaching about reading and what elementary teachers aren't learning*. Washington, DC: National Council on Teacher Quality. Available from: http://www.nctq.org

Waughn, S., & Ortiz, A. (n.d.). *Response to intervention in reading for English language learners*. Retrieved March 8, 2010, from http://www.rtinetwork.org/Learn/Diversity/ar/EnglishLanguage

Wayman, M. M., Wallace, T., Wiley, H. I., Ticha, R., & Espin, C. A. (2007). Literature synthesis on curriculum-based measurement in reading. *Journal of Special Education*, *41*(2), 85–120.

Weishaar, M. K. (2008). The law and reality: Understanding the Individuals With Disabilities Education Improvement

Act. In E. L. Grigorenko (Ed.), *Educating individuals with disabilities: IDEIA 2004 and beyond*. New York: Springer.

Weishaar, M. K., Borsa, J. C., & Weishaar, P. M. (2007). *Inclusive educational administration: A case study approach* (2nd ed.). Long Grove, IL: Waveland Press.

WETA. (n.d.). *Readability formulas: The Flesch reading ease readability formula*. Arlington, VA: Author. Retrieved December 3, 2009, from http://www.readability-formulas.com/flesch-reading-ease-readability-formula.php

WETA. (n.d.). *Readability formulas: The Fry graph readability formula*. Arlington, VA: Author. Retrieved November 23, 2009, from http://www.readabilityformulas.com/fry-graph-readability-formula.php

WETA. (n.d.). *Reading rockets: Teaching kids to read and helping those who struggle*. Arlington, VA: Author. Retrieved December 14, 2009, from http://www.readingrockets.org/

Will, M. C. (1986). Educating children with learning problems: A shared responsibility. *Exceptional Children, 53,* 411–415.

Zehr, M. A. (2010, January 10). Tailoring lessons for English-learners. *Education Week, 29*(19), 1, 10.

RESOURCES

General

Doing What Works: Research-Based Education Practices Online
- General content: Research-based practices, including data-driven improvement, quality teaching, literacy, math and science, comprehensive support, and early childhood
- Available at http://dww.ed.gov/
- See also What Works Clearinghouse, available at http://ies.ed.gov/ncee/wwc/

National Association of State Directors of Special Education
- General content: Policy and best practice on RTI
- Available at www.nasdse.org

National Research Center on Learning Disabilities
- General content: Policy and general information on specific learning disabilities and RTI
- Available at http://www.nrcld.org/topics/rti.html

RTI Wire
- General content: Overview of RTI, selecting interventions, working with teams, progress monitoring, developing graphs and charts
- Available at http://www.jimwrightonline.com/php/rti/rti_wire.php

Idea Partnership
- General content: Focus on students and youth with disabilities; includes links to RTI resources and evidence-based practices
- Available at http://www.ideapartnership.org/

RTI Action Network
- General content: Resources on quality instruction, interventions, assessment, and family involvement
- Available at http://www.rtinetwork.org/essential

Florida Center for Reading Research
- General content: Resources for teachers, coaches, administrators, parents, and researchers on core reading strategies, assessment programs, professional development, and interventions for readers who struggle
- Available at http://www.fcrr.org/index.shtml

Core Reading Program

University of Oregon
- General content: Information on evaluating and selecting a core reading program and general research-based programs and materials
- Available at http://reading.uoregon.edu/cia/curricula/index.php

Assessment

National Center on Student Progress Monitoring
- General content: Resources for families and professional development opportunities on progress monitoring
- Available at http://www.studentprogress.org/chart/chart.asp

Intervention Central
- General content: Easy-to-use CBM-based assessment tools; can generate CBM letter name fluency, wordlist fluency, reading fluency, and maze passage probes in reading; also houses tools for mathematics, writing, and behavior
- Available at http://www.interventioncentral.com/

National Center on Response to Intervention
- General content: Includes assessment tools, interventions, resources, and professional development opportunities
- Available at http://www.rti4success.org/
- For evaluation of progress monitoring tools in reading and math, see Tools/Interventions at http://www.rti4success.org/index.php
- For English language learners, see "Our Library" at http://www.rti4success.org/index.php

Intervention

RTI Tools
- General content: Provides resources for intervention strategies in reading, behavior, communication, writing, and mathematics as well as progress-monitoring tools and general information on RTI
- Available at http://www.rtitools.com/

Reading Rockets
- General content: Research-based ideas for reading interventions and activities for young children
- Available at http://www.readingrockets.org/

Phonemic awareness
- General content: Practical interventions supported by research for teachers
- See Scott, V. G. (2009). *Phonemic awareness: Ready-to-use lessons, activities, and games* (2nd ed.). Thousand Oaks, CA: Corwin Press.

Free Reading
- General content: Extensive lessons, ideas, and strategies for teaching reading between prekindergarten and sixth grade
- Available at http://www.free-reading.net/

Data-Based Decision Making

Practice Guide from What Works Clearinghouse
- General content: Schoolwide use of assessment data to support decision making
- Available at http://ies.ed.gov/ncee/wwc/pdf/practiceguides/dddm_pg_092909.pdf

INDEX